IN SEARCH OF PRIMAL

KNOWLEDGE

IN SEARCH OF PRIMAL

KNOWLEDGE

BY

ROBERT G. RAKESTRAW

ISBN: 1-58721-418-0

1stBooks – rev. 6/9/00

About the Book

This book is a dialogue - purportedly between the author and the readers - wherein the readers talk back to the author and discourse with each other about life, human creativity, men and women, government, society, the emotions, endorphins, pipe smoking, the carnal, the sensuous, and the celestial.

Primal Knowledge: the most important things we need to know about a subject in order to understand and deal with it.

-Robert G. Rakestraw

Chapter 1

Hello there, readers. Welcome to my book. I hope you enjoy our quest for primal enlightenment. As you will see, it is written in dialogue form--a dialogue purportedly between the author and the readers.

Have you ever wished, while reading a book, that you could talk back to the author? Discuss or argue some point with him? Well now you may--via the telepathic network--even as the book is being written. Of course, some of you might not be able to get through while the work is in progress. But don't let that possibility stop you from projecting an opinion or counter-argument. Although your ideas might not get printed in the book, they may show up anytime, even after the book is printed, whenever someone reads between the lines. As various readers join the dialogue, they will be referred to as Reader A, Reader B, and so forth.

READER A: (An insurance salesman): Okay, I'll go along with that. But first, what do you mean by primal knowledge?

AUTHOR: According to my Webster's dictionary, primal means first in time, first in rank, basic, fundamental, or first in importance. Knowledge is defined as a clear perception of a truth or fact.

In this undertaking, primal will refer, generally, to that which is basic or most important-- the most important things you need to know about a subject in order to understand and deal with it.

READER A: What are we going to be talking about?

AUTHOR: Whatever is of primal interest to the readers. Or we may seek basic information about subjects of merely secondary or tertiary interest.

READER A: Such as?

AUTHOR: Well, I don't wish to lay out the subjects. Let's go with the notion that primal truth, itself, wants to emerge, but that if we seek it too aggressively, it will pull itself in and close up like a terrapin or box turtle. On the other hand, if we proceed slowly and in a relaxed and loosely structured manner, truth like Br'er Terrapin, might poke its head out and then its feet and legs, and start crawling around, enabling us to observe it

READER A: You may have a point. So how should we proceed in order to keep Br'er Truth from sullin' up?

AUTHOR: Well, let's just ease into an everyday kind of subject. What are some of the things that are important to you-- or that you're interested in or concerned with?

READER A: Well, let's see. There's money, the opposite sex, sports. I'm particularly interested in running. I run several times a week. And I participate in an occasional 5 k or 10 k race.

AUTHOR: Speaking of running--can you tell me the difference between walking and running?

READER B {a full professor}: Oh--we're going to talk about running? If so, shouldn't you call your book *In Search of Trivial knowledge*? How can running be of primal interest to anyone?

AUTHOR: Well, I'd say that to a cave man fleeing from a jungle predator, the ability to run would have been of considerable importance. Anyway, I would still like an answer to my question.

READER A: Sure, I know the difference between walking and running. But first, tell me. What's the purpose of this search for primal knowledge?

AUTHOR: Good question. In baseball, a manager will tell you that to be successful in the game, you have to know what the fundamentals are. And you have to be able to execute them. So the purpose of this book is to search out and articulate the fundamentals of various aspects of the game of life, of the human condition, and various human activities and endeavors. On a particular subject, as you dig for that bit of primal knowledge, you can usually tell when you find it. The lamp of understanding clicks on. It is an exhilarating experience.

There's an awful lot of information extant in the world, today. And there are numerous ethical, religious, political, sociological, medical, artistic, aesthetic, and philosophical theories and systems, along with mountains of scientific

2

knowledge. You would think that the great minds of the world and the great leaders, in the various fields of endeavor, could get together and make some sense out of all this.

When you consider all the conflict, dysfunction, and plain stupidity rampant around the globe, and since the great ones among us are unable to agree on much of anything--much less solve the problems of the world--perhaps we ordinary folk should have a go at it. Is it not possible that the smartest people on earth might be among those who do not strive to reach alpine levels of accomplishment and prominence--and that the exalted ones are perhaps driven to such heights to compensate for a lack of good old common sense?

READER A: Hm-m. And how do we conduct this search? What is the process?

AUTHOR: Well, let's say the subject is running. And let's limit it to running by humans. First, let's name all the different types of running.

READER A: Well, there's jogging, trotting, loping, striding, and sprinting,

AUTHOR: Does walking come under running?

READER A: No, it's different.

AUTHOR: What is that difference?

READER A: Elementary--running is faster.

AUTHOR: Not necessarily. Isn't it possible for one person to jog along at a slower pace than someone who is walking fast?

READER A: Hm-m. Okay, how about this? Running uses more energy.

AUTHOR: A good point. Now if we can explain why running uses more energy than walking, we'll probably have the answer to our question.

READER A: That is the answer--as far as I can figure.

AUTHOR: Don't give up yet. I'm sure you can tell running from walking. My question, now, is how can you tell? Is it by intuitive insight or is it by intellectual analysis?

READER A: It's just common sense. When I was a child, I probably watched someone doing something that was referred to as running and someone else doing something referred to as

3

walking. And I can always tell the difference. I just can't say what the difference is.

AUTHOR: Hey, you've just come up with a brilliant explanation of the term "common sense".

READER A: I have?

AUTHOR: Yes, you just said that common sense is something you know, from experience, or that you can make a fairly accurate judgement on, even though you may not be able to delineate or articulate what it is you know.

READER A: Yeah, something like that.   Isn't that enough? Why do we have to get so technical?

AUTHOR: Well, for some people, climbing a mountain is exhilarating.   For others, discovering and articulating a new principle is an exciting thing. And such discoveries can, often times, be beneficial to mankind.

READER A: Are you some kind of an intellectual?

AUTHOR: No, no. An intellectual usually has a Ph D after his or her name. An intellectual knows just about everything there is to know in his field of endeavor--and an awful lot about everything else. I've always been interested in getting down to the basics, to the nitty gritty of things.

READER A: I had an uncle who was a Ph D. He was highly intelligent. His problem was that on most every day things he was just plain dumb.

AUTHOR: What you're saying is that intelligence doesn't necessarily include wisdom.

READER B: Or, as Heraclitus said, over two thousand years ago, "The learning of many things does not teach understanding."

AUTHOR: Thank you for that bit of input, Professor. Now, to get back to our subject. Let's try this: Get up from your chair, walk across the room, and then run back to your chair.

(READER A gets up, walks across the room, and runs back to his chair.)

READER A: The only difference I can tell is--as I said--running takes more energy.

AUTHOR: Well, let's break it down to single units. Do just one walking step and one running step. Slowly.

4

(READER A does as instructed.)

READER A: Seems to me the running step is more of a jump or leap.

AUTHOR: That's it! When you're walking, there is at least one foot on the ground, at all times. In running, both feet are off the ground at the same time, for a split second, on every step. Leaping defies gravity, thus takes more energy to perform. Just think--we may be the first to have defined this principle. It's a great feeling--isn't it?

READER B: Big deal--

READER A: Well, it's certainly a relief. I was beginning to feel a bit stupid. Now that we've got it, what good is it?

AUTHOR: It's primal knowledge. You lay it out on the table, and maybe, someday, someone will find a use for it. Perhaps a long distance runner will find a way to run more efficiently by using this information.   And, just think, henceforth, this may be referred to as the Author-Reader A principle!

READER A: Wouldn't that be something?

READER C (female aerobics instructor): Wait a minute, fellows. I hate to rain on your parade, but that information is already available, and has been for a long, long time. I explain it to my exercise classes, as a matter of course.

AUTHOR: Oh well, I'm really not surprised. And since we got in a little practice in searching for Primal Knowledge, our time wasn't wasted. Incidentally, I wonder if you can answer this question for me: What is the euphoric high some runners say they experience while running?

READER B: Endorphins.

READER C: I know what you're referring to, having felt it, myself, to some extent. But I don't know why it happens. Perhaps it relates back to the Stone Age. When your fleeing cave man sees that he's going to make it back safely to his cave he naturally begins to feel happy.

READER D (a couch-potato): The way I see it, people who run are engaged in self-torture. So, near the end of his run, the runner begins to anticipate the relief he'll feel when he stops running. It's like the man who was always hitting himself on the head with a hammer because it felt so good when he stopped.

READER B (the professor): I think I can explain it. What happens is this: when the fleeing cave man becomes exhausted and in pain--and is about to give up--his brain releases endorphins which smothers the pain and gives him a high, so that he can keep going until he gets back to his cave. It's designed to save his life.

AUTHOR: That is very informative, Professor, and very interesting. Are these endorphins released only to deal with pain? Or, can they be triggered by something else?

READER B: They just might be the source of all our pleasure and good feelings. Eating something we like might trigger their release. That would be nature's way of making sure we didn't starve to death. And sexual activity probably releases a flood of them to insure that we perpetuate our species. I don't know what the latest scientific data is on the subject. But it's a phenomenon, I feel, that warrants a great deal more attention.

AUTHOR: I agree. Perhaps we'll hear more about it from some of our readers, as we go along. One thing more--I'd like to bring up a philosophical question: Using walking and running as an analogy, is it better to walk through life and be content with minor achievements and moderate highs--or, is it better to race through life, seeking higher highs, grander trophies, and ever more impressive resumes, along with the attendant pain and stress?

READER A: Off hand, I'd say that is something each one of us must decide for himself. What I'd like to ask reader C is-- why can't I walk as fast as I can run?

READER C: I may have to get back to you on that question. However, it's probably that the length of a walking step is limited by the length of your legs. Whereas, the leaping step, in running, can be much longer, provided you have sufficient muscle power. As to the philosophical question, why not ask Reader D? Since he's not particularly interested in any form of self-locomotion, he should be able to come up with an unbiased answer.

READER D: My philosophy is--don't run or walk when you can sit, and don't sit when you can lie down.

Chapter 2

READER A: I agree, somewhat, with the professor that our subject in chapter one was a bit on the shallow side. When are we going to get into the deep stuff or, at least, something a little more sexy than running?

AUTHOR: When you use the word sexy, I presume you're speaking figuratively?

READER A: I think the Author just made a pun. Anyway, what I had in mind was something --anything--that will seize and hold on to the reader's attention. Sex is one such thing. You can't get much more primal than sex.

AUTHOR: I'm sure most people would agree with you on that. However, it has been scientifically proven that there is something infinitely more desirable and more enjoyable than sex, or food, or drink, and who knows what else. And I can't understand why the people, everywhere, aren't seeking it, with even more intensity and effort, than for anything else.

READER B {professor}:   What is it--baseball?

READER A: Only in Atlanta.

READER C {aerobics teacher}: It must be some kind of dope.

READER D {couch potato}: How about a good bowel movement?

READER E (young religious woman): Is it communion with God?

AUTHOR: Who knows? I'll tell you what was in the article, then you can speculate on your own. This is in reference to an actual laboratory experiment that was written up, a dozen or so years ago, in Harper's magazine. I thought, at the time, that it was a highly significant report, that would generate a tidal wave of comment, speculation, and wider experimentation. But I haven't seen or heard anything more about it. Of course there may have been follow-up reports on the subject. If there were, I haven't seen any of them.

Anyway, it seems this scientist was probing the brain of a mouse with a tiny wire that he would insert in different areas of the mouse's brain. For instance, when he inserted it in one place, and turned on a small amount of electrical current, the mouse would become very aggressive, baring his teeth and gnashing away at some phantom antagonist. And when he placed it in another area, the mouse would become extremely aroused, sexually. And in another place, withdrawn and depressed. And in another, ravenously hungry.

But, then, he inserted it in this one particular spot and the mouse seemed to become extremely pleased with himself, and appeared to be in a euphoric trance.

The scientist, wishing to find out more about the phenomenon, rigged up a device which, when the mouse pushed a tiny switch, would allow the mouse to receive three seconds of electrical stimulation to that area of his brain. The mouse quickly learned how to use it. As soon as the current would go off, the mouse would push the button again.

The scientist placed a female mouse, in heat, in with him, but he paid no attention to her and continued to push the button. And he would continue to do so until he passed out from exhaustion. Then, as soon as he returned to consciousness, he would take up where he'd left off.

READER A: But how do you know if it's applicable to humans?

AUTHOR: I don't know if it's been tried on any humans, yet. But the article further reports that the scientist, with the cooperation of the U.S. Army, rigged a device to an army pack mule. It was so arranged that if the mule kept moving in a certain direction he would receive the desired stimulation. But if he stopped or veered to the right or left, it would go off.

The mule kept going in the specified direction, over hill and dale. I suppose that the part of the brain being stimulated in the experiment was the area where endorphins are produced. Perhaps the Professor can shed some light on the subject.

READER B: I don't recall reading the Harper's article. I'll have to look it up. From what I've read about endorphins, there's at least seven different kinds. Some of them are several hundred times more powerful, as a pain killer, than morphine.

READER F (an artist): You don't know how excited I am to hear this subject brought up. I read that article and it nearly bowled me over.

The reason I was so impressed with the article was because once, when I was seven years old, I felt very intensely what that mouse must have been feeling. It was seemingly spontaneous and lasted about twenty or thirty minutes. And I agree with the mouse, it's better than anything else I ever experienced.

READER C: Can you describe the feeling and, also, tell us the circumstances that led up to your experience?

READER F: Well it was on a mild, sunny afternoon in February. My father had lost his job, in Arkansas, and we had come back to Georgia, around Christmas time, and had moved out on a farm. On this particular afternoon, I walked across the road and discovered a path leading up into the woods. The path was overgrown, in spots, with bushes and briars.

After following the path for a quarter of a mile or more, I came upon a small hollowed out spot, there in the middle of the woods. It was oval shaped and about twenty feet across. The ground was all packed down and the dirt was light colored. I contemplated the scene for a moment, wondering if it was a meeting place for the animals of the woods or, perhaps, for elves and fairies. There was no trash around.

Then, all of a sudden, this spell came over me. It seemed that I was encompassed with, and a part of, an intense feeling of love, understanding, meaningfulness, and spiritual oneness with God and the universe and with the past, present, and the future.

READER E: Seems to me you had a born again experience. Are you a Christian?

READER F: Partly. When I was a teenager, I got saved at a revival. But, now, I'm what you might call a backslider.

READER B: What led up to this? Were you running away from home? Had you been punished for something or denied something you wanted?

READER F: Not that. But I had been in a general state of uneasiness from having to adjust to a new school and new surroundings. After this happened, I felt much better from then on.

READER B: Have you ever discussed this with a professional person?

READER F: A few years ago, I discussed it with a minister and asked him what he thought it was. He didn't seem to be impressed with what I'd told him and didn't offer any explanation or speculation as to what it might be.

Then, not long ago, I discussed it with a psychiatrist and asked him what it was all about. His response delivered in a casual manner, was that I'd had a brain spasm. When I asked him what might have triggered it, he said he didn't know.

READER E: Is your psychiatrist an atheist?

READER F: He's not my psychiatrist. I struck up a conversation with him at an art exhibit. And no, he's not an atheist--I think he's a Presbyterian.

READER A: The preacher and the psychiatrist were just being polite. They just didn't want to tell you that what you experienced was a case of temporary insanity.

READER D: Don't pay any attention to Reader A. Here is what really happened, folks. Reader F walks up this path, pushing past bushes and briars, stepping over fallen logs, and suddenly comes to this nice cozy peaceful little hollow. <u>He's back in the womb</u>. Safe and secure.

Perhaps what he's feeling is what he felt when he first became conscious. Just imagine how you must have felt, for the very first time, coming out of the void into the consciousness of being alive.

READER B: Becoming aware of being alive is most likely a very gradual thing. It might begin with conception. But according to scientific theory, the primal layer of consciousness, even after birth, deals mostly with hunger, thirst, breathing, elimination, touch, loud noises, and falling.

The second layer, having to do with emotional awareness, starts functioning at about six months after birth.

And the third layer, having to do with intellectual understanding, ideation, and creativity, kicks in at our around age five.

READER E: To be "born again" in Christ is to become suddenly aware of an even higher consciousness. Can anyone prove to the contrary that what Reader F felt was direct contact with the Supreme Being? Or that there is a portion of the brain that was created just for that purpose? I think not.

And, moreover, is it not possible that each cell in the human body may contain receptors capable of receiving and responding to the emanations of God's will and the Holy Spirit--and that the key to this joyous experience is faith, expressed through prayer?

AUTHOR: Wow! This discussion is getting to be quite heady. When I first thought of writing this book, it was because I thought I had pretty well figured out what life--from a practical standpoint-- was all about. And I wanted to share my great insights with everyone else, in the form of a book of little essays on the various aspects of life.

But then I came up with the idea that, instead of essays, it might be more effective and entertaining to write it in dialogue form, a dialogue between the author and the readers. The upshot of it is that your contributions have been so sharp and have been so well articulated that I've become a bit intimidated--even though I know that you are only creatures of my imagination.

READER D: I wouldn't be too sure about that.

AUTHOR: I'm not really sure about anything, anymore.

READER B: Join the club. I think I speak for many when I say, the more you learn, the more you realize how much you don't know and less sure you are of what you thought you knew.

READER A: Or as John F. Kennedy put it: "The more our knowledge increases, the more our ignorance unfolds."

READER D: We are never going to get a clear explanation of existence. The Man Upstairs knows better than to let that happen. We'd be bored to death. Just how long do you think anyone would watch a soap opera if there were no misunderstandings, no stupidity, no neurotics, no good guys, no bad guys, no suspense, no conflicts, or no catastrophes?

So maybe you don't have all the answers. Neither does anyone else. *Alfie* can't tell us what it's all about. Not even Hugh Downs can explain it. The way I figure, I have as much right to make a fool of myself as anyone else. The main thing is not necessarily to find, but to seek.

Author: After listening to Reader F and Sister E, all of you for that matter, it seems more likely than ever, to me, that there is a higher intelligence out there--someone or some thing that knows what creation is all about. And how it came to be, and what's right and what's wrong.

READER B: To answer Reader E's question: No, we can't prove one way or the other that what Reader F felt was direct contact with God.

Now, I would like to raise a question. Could it be that the euphoria center of the brain is the progenitor of the idea of a supreme being--and that it's the driving force behind all the different religions?

READER F: You may be on to something, Professor. At least, it may be the source of the idea of Heaven. I've often thought that what I felt, that day, is what it would feel like to be in Heaven. Most people have a vague idea of what Heaven might be like. And even though they may not expect any earthly pleasures there--such as food, sex or whatever--they still want to go there.

I don't think I'm unique in all this. There must be others who've had a similar experience. And maybe they'll join our dialogue, as we go along, and tell us all about it. I hope so.

READER C: It seems to me that in our search for primal knowledge, we're about to go off the deep end. Can we change the subject? Something a little more practical?

READER A: Yeah. But before we do that, let's do some reviewing. In chapter one we learned the difference between walking and running. And, so far, in chapter two, we've learned that, sometimes, it's fun to be crazy. Anything else?

READER B: My, My! The way you cut to the bare bones of something is astounding. Tell me, Reader A, what do you think happens when an individual dies?

READER A: Well, if he's properly insured, his family will be well taken care of.

AUTHOR: On that high note, let's bring this chapter to a close and go on to chapter three, perhaps, as Reader C suggests, to a more practical subject.

Chapter 3

READER G: (newspaper reporter): May I bring up a subject for discussion? It's something everyone should find useful as well as interesting.

AUTHOR: And what might that be?

READER G: The art of writing. As a reporter, I'm naturally interested in the subject and curious as to what is the most important thing to keep in mind, when writing. Also, I'm curious to see how you go about stripping away that which is less than primal and coming down to the number one thing.

AUTHOR: Very well. It's a subject I find particularly fascinating. And, I can certainly use any good pointers we might come up with. For a starter, let's define writing.

READER C {aerobics teacher}: Writing is a form of communication.

READER D {couch potato}: Writing is entertainment.

AUTHOR: Communication, I would say, is the prime reason for writing. And entertainment is one of the things we might want to communicate through the medium. However, I think what we are searching for, in this instance, has to do with the make-up or the ingredients.

READER B {professor}: From a technical standpoint, writing is the use of configurative symbols for the spoken word.

READER H (musician): And for any kind of sounds, such as music, animal sounds, sounds made by machines, noises, and so forth.

READER G: Also for silences and for accents, stress, and emphasis - as indicated by punctuation marks.

READER C: The answer is simple: the prime ingredient is words.

READER G: Yeah--but you just can't dump words onto a piece of paper and call it literature.

AUTHOR: How about content or meaningfulness.

READER B: Not necessarily. Take, for example, the nonsense bit from *Through the Looking Glass*, by Lewis Carroll:

"Twas brillig, and the slithy toves
Did gyre and gimble in the wabe.
All mimsy were the boro goves
And the mome raths out grabe."

To me that's an entertaining bit of writing. But I wouldn't call it especially meaningful. What we're looking for is something that is applicable to all forms of writing, whether it's a novel, an essay, poetry, advertising copy, a slogan, or a letter to your grandmother.

READER D: It's the way you put the words together - the arrangement. The way it sounds to the inward ear. For example: in the movie, *Casablanca*, when Ingrid Bergman says: "Play it, Sam--"at that particular point in the story, it says so much with so little. It's the perfect selection and arrangement of words. In fact, if you try to substitute any other name in place of Sam, the whole effect goes out the window. "Play it Jack" or "Play it Sidney, George, or William" just wouldn't have the same effect. Why is that?

READER B: Yes. On the surface, "Play it Sam" would seem to be an order or a command. A phrase that begins with an accented syllable and ends with an accented syllable is usually bold and assertive in nature. But since Sam is a long sounding syllable--almost a diphthong--the effect turns out to be somewhat ambivalent. It starts off as assertiveness and ends up as something else--resignation with a bit of poignancy thrown in.

READER C: If I remember correctly, what Miss Bergman said to Dooley Wilson was: Play it once, Sam--"

READER D: Picky, Picky. There you go again--putting the cake out in the rain.

READER C: Don't burst a couch spring, Reader D. I was just stating a fact. Anyway, I think your way sounds better. And I agree with you and the Professor about the effect the word "Sam" has on the phrase. I think the "S" in Sam is involved: it adds a sigh-like sound to the phrase--a sigh of resignation, so to speak.

READER D: It does indeed. And you were right about the wording. I remember the whole bit, now: "Play it once, Sam--for old time's sake. Play *As Time Goes By*--

READER H: And I suppose the second phrase, "For old time's sake," could evoke a twinge of poignancy: it might reverberate in the mind as "Old time's ache." Ache as in heartache.

AUTHOR: Your implication is that a word can evoke an emotion not normally associated with the word itself, just because of it's similarity, in sound, to some other word.

READER H: What we're talking about is cadence. Take the phrase "Tom, Dick, and Harry." No matter how you rearrange it, you can't make it sound better. Somehow, "Dick, Harry, and Tom" or "Harry, Tom, and Dick" just doesn't have the right swing to it..

READER R: The general rule is that in a series, such as "Tom, Dick, and Harry," the longest word should be last. The same thing applies to a series of phrases, such as: "I came, I saw, I conquered"--the longest phrase should be last.

READER C: Speaking of Tom, Dick, and Harry - I think those three fellows used to work out at my health club. Tom was <u>tall</u>, Dick was <u>dark</u>, and Harry was <u>handsome</u>.

AUTHOR: "Tall, dark, and handsome"--"Tom, Dick, and Harry." Isn't that amazing? Two well known phrases have the exact same cadence. Furthermore, each accented syllable in the two phrases begins with the same letter.

READER A: There's also: "Stop, Look, and Listen" and "Hook, Line, and Sinker." Just proves you can't keep a good cadence down. In regard to the professor's rule about putting the longest word, or the longest phrase, last--there's at least one exception to that rule. In the old baseball phrase--"Tinker, To Evers, To Chance"--the last word has only one syllable. Yet the phrase really swings.

READER D: Well, that's because it fits the action of the double-play. The excitement starts at the shortstop position, builds at second base, and comes to a sharp climax at first. In all likelihood, if Chance had played shortstop and Tinker had played first base, all three players would have been virtually forgotten, by now. "Chance, to Evers, to Tinker" is a clinker. Edgar Guest would never have used it in a poem.

AUTHOR: Well, let's see what we have here. Writing is a process of using configurative symbols for various accented sounds, unaccented sounds, and silences, which are arranged by the author to convey his ideas and feelings.

Of course, there are other important elements, such as content, imagery, alliteration, metaphor, simile, syntax, logic, grammar, exposition, dialogue, and the technical things - such as paragraphs, sentences, phrases, words, syllables, punctuation, and so forth. But I think we agree that the rhythmic arrangement of sounds and silences--the cadence--is the primal thing. This is true whether you're writing an essay, a news story, a bumper sticker - or a letter to the professor's grandmother.

READER C: I've always heard that writing has to flow.

READER D: True. But, that's not to say that it mayn't crash into and around boulders in the stream, leap over falls, race through narrow channels, or spin off into digressive eddies, as it flows onward to the main.

AUTHOR: Understood, I'm sure.

READER G: To put it another way: in every example of effective writing there is a current that grabs the reader, at the start, and takes him in tow on an exciting, well structured journey down a stream that flows from the writer's conscious. Depending on the effectiveness of the writing and the responsiveness of the reader, the result, at the end of the journey, is that the reader has been informed, entertained, inspired, or persuaded to think or act in a certain way.

AUTHOR: In light of our discourse here on the importance of phrasing, and cadence, and flow, I'm afraid I might have to go back and do some major revising of this book. What do you think?

READER F: The title's not bad. Catchy, in fact. But, as to your opening sentence, "Hello Readers--welcome to my book" the best I can say for it is that it's polite and friendly.

READER D: I'll have to admit, it's no "Call me Ishmael." But it does set the stage for the dialogue between the author and the readers--like a talk show host welcoming his panel of quests.

READER B: The rhythm's okay. You might say it's a triumph of cadence over content. But that might also be said of "Once upon a time."

READER E {young religious woman}: My favorite opening sentence is, "In the beginning, God created the heavens and the earth".

READER A: The most under-rated, probably, is "It was a dark and stormy night". If it's as bad as they say, how come it's so well remembered?

READER G: A moment ago, Reader D mentioned "Call me Ishmael", from *Moby Dick*. As you savor this first morsel, served up by Mr. Melville, you know right away that you're in for a literary feast. In the same league with it is Dickens's "It was the best of times, it was the worst of times", from *A Tale of Two Cities*, which also has a great ending.

READER H: "It is a far, far better thing that I do, than I have ever done: it is a far, far better rest that I go to, than I have ever known."

READER G: Warm and comforting--like a glass of peach brandy.

AUTHOR: I wonder how much time he spent on that one sentence. I wonder if he considered leaving out the word "that" and writing, "It is a far, far better thing. I do," instead. And if he did consider it, why did he chose to leave it in?

READER B: Wouldn't it be interesting to go back in time and discuss it with him?

READER; I   (A gentleman dressed in nineteenth century garb): Hello, fellow readers, I thank you for the kind remarks about my writing.

READER B: Mr. Dickens! What are you doing here? Isn't the latter part of the twentieth century a bit after your time?

READER I: Call me the Ghost of Century Past. Or you can call me Ghost Writer, if you like. Or Ghost Reader for that matter. As to the Author's question about the closing sentence in *A Tale of Two Cities*: yes, more than a little time was spent shaping and polishing it. As for the word "that," it's used for a purpose, both times that it appears. My natural inclination is to make my writing sound musical. Read it again--and listen as you read. Those two "thats" are delicate little drum taps..

Listen, also, to the words "do" and "done"--the way they fit in.

The last part of the sentence was the more difficult to handle. For instance: "It is a far, far better rest that I go to, than I have ever <u>experienced</u>": would not, I'm sure, satisfy Reader D's inward ear. And "It is a far, far better rest that I go to, then I have ever <u>had</u>", sounds even worse. Thank goodness for the word "known". It's the perfect word I needed to end the sentence. It sets just the right tone. And notice the subtle harmonic relationship between the word "known" and the word "done", which comes at the end of the first part of the sentence.

I hope that satisfies your curiosity about my writing style. Now, I'm afraid I must leave you. I'm beginning to fade. Farewell…

AUTHOR and READERS: Goodbye, Mr. Dickens-

READER G: After listening to Charles Dickens' comments, there is another aspect of writing that we should emphasize. It has to do with the character and tone of a word as determined by the arrangement of the vowels and consonants that comprise it and how it fits in, tonally, with other words in a phrase or sentence. It's akin to shading and color in painting. Harmony and dissonance in music.

AUTHOR: An unarguable point, Reader G.

Chapter 4

READER J {bartender}: Hey, you people, I've been enjoying the conversation. There's something I'd like to bring up, if I may. It has to do with my job as a bartender. I often have customers who seem to want to use me as a substitute psychiatrist. They tell me their problems and ask for advice.

READER A {insurance man}: What sort of problems?

READER J: Generally, they have to do with personal relationships of one kind or another--problems with the girlfriend or boyfriend, spouse or other family members, or on-the-job relationships.

READER A: Do you ever give any advice to the customers?

READER J: Not much--except to advise them when they've had too much to drink. Most of the time, I just listen and try to say something comforting or consoling. Something that, along with the alcohol, will lift their spirits. The reason I don't offer any advice is because I don't have any to give that I'm real sure of. But if you fellows can come up with some of this primal knowledge that's relevant, maybe I can pass it along.

AUTHOR: We can try. Is there a particular subject you'd like to tackle first?

READER J: Yes. It's the tough one. You know--the man-woman relationship. I don't know how many women there are who understand men, but there are a whole bunch of men out there who don't know beans about women. They either try to dominate the woman completely, or they knuckle under completely--or they avoid them altogether.

READER A: Do you have any ideas of your own? Or a suggestion as to how we might approach it?

READER J: Well, yes I have this one idea. It's kinda crazy, but it may be a start. It has to do with the seamier side of life, the so-called baser_instincts, and specifically with what goes on in joints --gambling joints, gin joints, drug houses, whorehouses, and what have you.

For instance, prostitution is referred to as the world's oldest profession. And, usually, we think of it as men paying women

21

for sex. From this we can assume that, since the beginning of recorded history or before, men have had an appetite for sex on demand, and women have a strong desire for money. What is the significance of this?

READER A: The way I see it, in order to insure perpetuation of the species, Mother Nature gave the male the ever present desire to have his way with any nubile person of the opposite sex that comes his way. And to make sure that any offspring that might result has a chance to grow up, Mother Nature gave the female a strong desire for security--a safe place to bring up the young one and the wherewithal for food, clothing and so forth.

READER C {female aerobics teacher}: That's a crude way to put it. But I suppose the money the prostitute gets could conceivably represent material security. Now, if we can figure out how this fits in with civilized society, and with the phenomenon of falling in love, and with the institution of marriage, we might come up with some primal insight that Reader J can pass on to his bar clients.

READER D {couch potato}: Okay. If we accept Reader A's premise, let's first try to ascertain what your normal average woman would want in the way of security.

READER C: To feel secure, most women would like a nice home in a nice, safe neighborhood. A faithful husband who is a good, protective provider, who is a responsible, up-standing citizen; and who is well thought of in his community; and is one who is considerate and generous, and who remembers birthdays and anniversaries; and who spends time with the children.

READER A: How about adequate insurance, or an investment folio, or a retirement plan?

READER C: That too.

READER D: You didn't mention that he should always be home by five-thirty or six. And that he should be nice to his mother-in-law and the rest of his wife's family--and not too involved with his own family.

AUTHOR: Okay, let's don't attempt to enumerate every little detail. As I see it, there are four basic kinds of security that women are concerned with: first, financial security; second, physical safety for herself, her family, and her community; third, a secure position as a respected member of a loving and appreciative family; and fourth, a secure status as an accepted member of her community.

READER J: Wouldn't these things apply to men as well as women?

READER G {newspaper man}: To a certain extent, but it's been my observation that security is not the prime concern or motivation for men. Whereas, for women, I believe security is the number one motivation.

READER J: If that is true, then why do some women attach themselves to abusive, no-good bums?

READER C: In some instances, a lonely, naive woman gets taken in by a glib, lying charmer who later turns out to be a lousy rat instead of the loving, protective winner that she had presumed him to be.

Then, there are other women who have a very low sense of self-worth and are self-destructive. They do things and put up with things that are just the opposite of what is good for them or for their offspring.

As children, we learn very quickly not to touch something that is dangerously hot. But some women get burned in one relationship after another. Either that, or they destroy one relationship after another because of that same feeling of unworthiness or from an irrational and inflated sense of insecurity.

READER J: What's behind these feelings of insecurity and low self-esteem? Is it because of bad things that have happened to them--or that have been done to them, over the years?

READER C: Very likely. Also it could stem from bad choices that they themselves have made.

READER D: Are you implying that we should not construe, in every case, that a man was the cause of it all?

READER C: Not in every case. But we should consider the possibility of it.

AUTHOR: A moment ago, Reader G stated that security is not the prime concern or motivation for men. Then what is? What word best describes it?

READER E {young religious woman}: Conquest.

READER G: Well, what I had in mind was achievement or accomplishment.

AUTHOR: As I see it, there's not that much difference between conquest and achievement. Each involves doing what one sets out to do.

READER C: I think conquest is more apt than achievement because of the male's will {fueled by testosterone} to dominate.

AUTHOR: Isn't it possible that a man's desire to achieve or dominate is motivated by an overall concern of security for himself and his family?

READER C : For some men, perhaps. For others it's just an excuse. They like to climb a mountain just because it's there; or shoot a deer or a dove just for the sport of it. They like to compete, whether it's in the business world, the playing field, or the battlefield, just for the sake of winning. They even do it vicariously, by watching sports on the television or at various sports arenas.

READER D: Speaking of domination, does everyone agree with the Bible that, in marriage relationships, the husband should lead and the woman dutifully follow?

READER C: No--at least not unconditionally.

READER B {professor}: I think I may have the answer to that question. And I didn't come by it academically--it's my own common sense conclusion, drawn from experience.

As a young man, I was enrolled by my parents in Miss Mason's ballroom dancing class. Even though Miss Mason was very strict as to behavior and dress, I took to ballroom dancing avidly. I still remember the first time I put my arm around a girl's waist and how soft and pleasant it felt.

Later on, I helped pay my way through college by teaching ballroom dancing.

Anyway, what I discovered is that in ballroom dancing, the man and woman don't move exactly in unison as, let's say, the Rockettes do. To dance in unison you'd have to remember an exact routine. That would be boring. It's much more fun when the man leads the woman and the woman puts up some resistance {but not too much} and follows the man through the

24

steps. The woman should not try to anticipate the next step--that would result in unison movement. She should hold back a little so that the man has to nudge her along.

READER C: I'll have to admit that just about every woman who likes to dance appreciates a good strong leader for a partner--but only if he keeps in time with the music and is not a jerk or slob.

READER H {musician}: As I see it the boys follow the music, the girls follow the boys, and the musicians follow the girls.

READER B: I also came to the conclusion that in dancing {and in other things as well}, the woman leads in a negative way. If a man is rushing the music, she can slow him down. And if he just can't follow the music at all, or if he keeps stepping on her toes {or is a jerk}, she can refuse to dance with him.

READER A: I see. In dancing or in other aspects of the relationship, the man is in charge as long as he does things her way.

READER B: Something like that. Also there are a few men who, although they may be tigers in the business world, appear to be the next thing to a wimp on the dance floor. And any women who wants to dance with them might wind up having to lead.

READER C: On the other hand, some men who are weak and ineffectual in most situations in life, become the essence of manly charm, grace, and leadership once they get on the dance floor.

READER D: Well, the reason for that is--dancing is part of the make-believe world, like acting, or writing, or painting, or music. Some people who aren't too good at battling it out in the real world, or in the business of raising a family, or of getting along with people, do it vicariously {sometimes very convincingly} in their make-believe endeavors.

AUTHOR: These are all interesting points--but I think it's about time that we brought this subject to a close.

READER C: Not yet. We haven't discussed what it is a man looks for in a woman--other than slavish adoration.

READER D: An adoring slave sums it up pretty well. Also, she needs to be a nurturing, caring mother to his little ego boosting tax-deductions--otherwise known as children.

And, as with his other trophies, she must keep herself shined up--well groomed and beautiful--especially when he wants to display her to his friends and business associates.

READER A: And if she wants to help with the family income by working outside the home, it's okay as long as she continues to serve him his meals on time, take care of the kids, and keeps the house clean.

READER H: And in the bedroom, she should be tantalizing, seductive, and headache-free. And as the professor said, the woman should resist a little--but not too much.

AUTHOR: Very well put, gentlemen. As, I'm sure, our distaff members will agree.

READER C: That's what they'd like, I'm sure.

AUTHOR: Has anyone else noticed that, in this chapter, we seemed to have reversed our normal process? Previously, we peeled off the outside layers of the subject until we got down to the basic parts. This time, I believe, we came up with the prime ingredients at the very beginning, then added on more.

However, we still haven't addressed the phenomenon of falling in love or the institution of marriage.

READER A: I've often heard--and you probably have, too-- that the condition of being in love is just another example of temporary insanity. Sounds plausible. Because, when you're in love, there's no way the object of your affection can be as perfect and as wonderful as you perceive her or him to be. This becomes evident when the effect wears off. Nature's purpose in this is to make the couple cling to each other long enough, time-wise, for the relationship to become a habit, or at least until their offspring are up and running around.

READER B: As for the institution of marriage, that is society's way of dealing with the same thing, a matter of promoting a long lasting relationship between the man and the woman, and a stable environment in which to bring up the little ones.

26

READER E: True marriages are made in Heaven. God makes a free gift of that first outpouring of love between the two. But afterwards, they must work to keep that love flowing by remaining committed to each other and by seeking and following God's plan for them.

AUTHOR: I think that we can agree that the more love, understanding, consideration, and commitment both parties can bring to the relationship, the longer it will last and the better it will be. And that the instant gratification sought in prostitution or one-night stands only short circuits the process of forming worthwhile relationships.

READER C: Yes. And if two people beginning a relationship would spend more time getting to know each other and each other's families and friends, and in doing things together before they go hopping into bed, they'd have a much better chance at coming up with a satisfying, long lasting relationship.

READER D: To put it another way--make it a point to become soul mates before you become bed mates.

READER J: I would like to make a couple of comments to go with the keen points you've expounded. For one thing, neither party in a relationship ought to expect his partner--or himself--to be a model of perfection. However, it's reasonable to expect the man to be something more than a braying jackass and for the woman to be more than a nagging, whining female canine.

The other point is that both had better have a sense of humor, to get them over the rough spots.

AUTHOR: Well taken--on both points. To sum up, now: In the way of primal knowledge, I think we agree that, in general, men are motivated by the desire to achieve, conquer, and to dominate. And women are motivated by the desire for security and by the desire to nurture.

READER D: Sometimes, however, the opposite occurs. And when it occurs in a man, he's called a wimp. And when it occurs in a woman, she's referred to as a dragon lady.

READER C: I think Reader J should advise his troubled customers that partners in a relationship should become aware of

27

each other's basic motivations; be reasonably considerate of each other's desires and needs; they should be loving, affectionate, and faithful; and they should help each other in the pursuit of worthy goals and endeavors.

READER G: The big question is: How can we deal with the emotional hang-ups and other problems stemming from the past? I'm talking about the poisonous residue--from bad experiences, bad behavior, and bad choices--that every now and then bubbles up into the present and screws things up.

READER B: Philosophers, religious leaders, poets, physicians, and psychologists have been seeking the answer to that question for a long, long time. Many of them believe they have the solution and that the only real problem is getting people to subscribe to their particular nostrum, treatment, incantation, creed, or dogma.

READER D: They may all be right. In minor cases, where the problem isn't deeply rooted, a couple of drinks at Reader J's bar and yakking with someone about what's bothering you might be enough to get you back into your little darling's arms.

But for the tough cases you need a much stiffer libation--like the one I heard about on T.V. It's called the connubial cocktail.

READER J: I don't believe I've ever heard of that one.

READER D: Well, that's because it requires a different assortment of spirits than the ones you dispense.

If I remember correctly, you start with a spoonful of kindness, add a jigger of faith, a dollop of understanding, a twist of humor, then fill to the brim with love--and garnish with enthusiasm. And according to the fellow on T.V., it works like a charm--and there's never a hangover.

READER J: Hm-m. I'd better write that down. Let's see-- one spoonful of kindness, a jigger of faith, a dollop of......

Chapter 5

READER K (a farmer): If you folks don't mind, I'd like to tell you about an experience I had similar to the one Reader F told you about in chapter two. The euphoria thing. I never had the nerve to tell anyone about it, before. But since Reader F told his story--I say, what the heck.

AUTHOR: We'd be happy to hear it, I'm sure. And it should be interesting to compare it with Reader F's experience.

READER K: This happened a long time ago, when I was about seventeen or eighteen years old. We had a large vegetable garden on the other side of a wooded hill, about a quarter of a mile from the house. The garden was in a level spot--surrounded on three sides by sloping hills, forming a kind of natural amphitheater.

I had gone over to the garden to pick green beans for my mother to can. The weather was hot and sultry and the whole time I was picking beans, mosquitoes were feasting on me--that is until the last few minutes. Then all of a sudden, I noticed they had quit biting me and in fact had disappeared.

I picked up the basket of beans and went over to the edge of the woods and sat down to rest and cool off in the shade. It was then that I became aware of this terrific feeling of euphoria coming over me. Much like the way Reader F described his experience--the meaningfulness, the great understanding, the feeling of being at one with the universe, past, present and future. With one slight difference. Whereas his was kinda peaceful like, my experience was real glorious, as if angelic choirs were singing, up above the tall pines that I was sitting under. It was as if Heaven, itself, had been brought down close to the earth.

I've wondered, all these years, about what it was that was going on. I suppose--like Reader F--I might have had a brain spasm. At the time, I thought that God had just taken a notion to intervene between me and the mosquitoes and to shed a little grace on me.

READER D (couch potato): How big were these mosquitoes?

READER K: They were just your ordinary regular sized mosquitoes.

READER D: Out our way, we have some extra large jumbo size mosquitoes. What might have happened is that one of these suckers might have strayed over into your neck of the woods, chased off your mosquitoes, and bit you on the top of the head, penetrating your skull and hitting the euphoria area of your brain--triggering your happy spell.

READER K: Well, I don't know about that.

READER B (professor): Perhaps there's a logical reason why the mosquitoes quit biting you. Maybe the advent of a stiff, sustained breeze caused them to stop, or some other atmospheric change--or even the time of day.

READER A (insurance man): Yeah. It could have been their nap time.

AUTHOR: Although we can't say, for sure, what caused the mosquitoes to suddenly cease biting Reader K, can we assume that the fact that they did is what triggered the euphoric experience?

READER K: Maybe. But there's a possibility that the spasm, or whatever it was, was underway before the mosquitoes stopped biting me--and that when you're under a spell like this, you are protected from anything harmful or unpleasant.

READER A: Seems to me that could be determined, scientifically, by planting an electrode in the euphoria center of someone's brain and then putting him in a room full of mosquitoes.

READER G (reporter): Perhaps the scientist that was mentioned in chapter two could test it out on a mouse first--that is, if mosquitoes bite mice.

READER K: While he's at it, he might hook up the device to another one of those army mules to see if it will repel horseflies.

READER C (aerobics instructor): I wonder if this euphoric state can be invoked through hypnosis? If so, you could do all sorts of tests, such as testing one's resistance to heat or cold, caustic substances, poisons, or to physical stress and so forth.

READER G: What I'd like to know is: what has that scientist been doing in the way of follow up, since the mouse experiments? Has he tried it on a human, yet?

READER A: You're the reporter. Look up the scientist and interview him. Volunteer to be a guinea pig. I'm sure your editor would give you expense paid time off to pursue such a story.

READER G: He would probably give me a funny look.

READER F (artist): By the way, although I've had only that one super-duper euphoric experience, that I told you about in chapter two, every now and then I'll feel a milder version of it, brought on by such things as a change in the season, or a nice sunset, or when a painting I'm working on turns out the way I wanted it to. It's a very pleasant <u>all's right with the world</u> sort of feeling.

I suppose everyone has that experience, once in a while--that is if they can throttle down their every day concerns long enough for it to seep through. Does anyone know what I'm talking about?

AUTHOR: I think I do. Sometimes, early in the morning, when I go out to get the paper, and things are still relatively quiet, I can hear doves cooing down by the Walnut street bridge. The sound they make evokes a feeling of kinship, not only with the dove but with the rest of creation as well.

This only happens when I can, as you say, throttle down. Even then, it's usually faint and elusive.

READER A: The thing that can give me that kind of feeling is when I smack a golf ball just right, off the tee, and it just keeps going and going, seemingly headed for infinity.

READER H (musician): Probably the easiest and the most universally effective way to experience the phenomenon is to look into a pair of friendly eyes. There's some kind of wordless communication that goes on between yourself and the other person. And it doesn't matter what the age of the other person is. The communication can be just as strong with a one year old child or with an octogenarian, as it is with some one your own age.

They say the eyes are the windows of the soul. When the eyes I contact are friendly, it seems to me that I'm not only in communication with the soul behind those eyes but also, to some extent, with a universal soul.

READER G (reporter): What happens if the eyes you look into are unfriendly?

READER H: That happens--and when it does, I get a feeling of hostility and tension. Not very pleasant.

Some eyes seem to project sorrow and sadness. Sometimes the sadness and sorrow seems deep and painful. Other times, it's a mild sweet sadness--like that engendered by the sound of mourning doves. With some eyes there seems to be no communication--no connection.

READER B: Have you thought about what part facial expression might play in what is communicated?

READER H: Yeah, I've wondered about that. To find out, I guess you'd have to put someone behind a curtain with holes cut to show the eyes.

It might be that you would get a connection but no specific emotional communication.

READER D: My, my! Aren't we getting inspirational? That's okay--I love inspiration. Any number of old movies from the thirties and forties can put me in that mellow mood. *Bahama Passage*, with Madalyn Carroll and Sterling Hayden, is one of my favorites. It's about sailing and falling in love. Another is *Captains Courageous*, with Spencer Tracy, Freddie Bartholomew, and Mickey Rooney. And of course there's *Casablanca*.

READER C: I suppose I'm different from you guys. What affects me in a meaningful way is when I do something worthwhile or help someone in need. Or when I create or promote a feeling of well being. Or when I observe someone else doing these things.

AUTHOR: From what I'm hearing, it seems we can come by this good feeling by doing something well or something worthwhile. Or passively, by giving our attention to some certain thing outside ourselves.

We all seem to recognize this feeling. Just what is it? What do we call it?

READER E (young, religious woman): It's true pure love. Spiritual--not sensual. In the Holy Bible, it says: "God is love." So, what you've felt is the Holy Spirit, which, as I said, is true pure love.

READER G: Does the bible tell you how to plug into this source?

READER E: That's the whole purpose of the Bible, whether by inspiration, as from the Psalms, the Teachings of Jesus .and other bible stories. Or by admonition, as from the Ten Commandments, Proverbs, and, again, the Teachings of Christ.

One particular verse I like is: "Be still and know that I am God."

READER G: That's similar to what was said earlier--about throttling down. But how about the last part: "and know that I am God?" Does that mean that if you become still, mentally and physically, that you will experience the spirit of God?

READER E: Perhaps. Or it might be simply an exhortation to stop and acknowledge the Great Creator, the Higher Intelligence, The Supreme Being. I think that if we all did this, several times a day, we'd feel better, look better, and do better.

READER D: In other words, if you are feeling worn out from the rat race--or down from watching that calvacade of sleaze, degradation, stupidity, and violence known as the evening news, you should take the time to, as they say, stop and smell the roses--and thank God for them.

READER C: In your case, you'll have to extricate yourself from that couch, turn off the T.V. and go outside to where thee roses are.

READER D: Couldn't I just have them brought in and perhaps sniff them during the commercials?

33

Chapter 6

READER A {insurance man}: Okay, we've stopped and smelled the roses. Now, it's time to wake up and smell the coffee

I'm talking about government, the United States government in particular. It's gotten to where people have to work from January first on into the month of May just to pay their taxes. And if William and Hillary Rodham Clinton had had their way, back in 1993, by now, we'd be working well into June or July before we could earn any money for ourselves.

Author: Are you referring to the push toward more socialism as evidenced by the defunct 1993 Clinton health care plan?

READER A: If you ask me, it was more like fascism, as practiced by Benito Mussolini. Incidentally, the arrogant way Mr. Clinton sticks out his lower jaw, at times, reminds me of the late dictator.

AUTHOR: You seem quite passionate about this. Can you be more specific?

READER B: {professor}: I think what had him worried was the effect the Clinton plan would have had on the insurance business.

READER A: Damn right. All that talk about a single payer system suggests to me that he was out to do in the health insurance business as well as wreak the health-care system. Fortunately the public woke up in time and stopped it.

I thought the Republican victories in the 1994 elections had put the kibosh on big government. However, thanks to a Joseph Goebbels type propaganda barrage of lies, misrepresentation, and demonization by the liberals in the congress, and elsewhere, against the Republicans, Clinton got reelected, in 1996, and he is now trying to win incrementally what he was unable to get in one fell swoop, back in '93.

READER L [conservative businessman]: In their hearts the voters know that the Republicans are right about shrinking the federal government. That's why they kept them in charge of congress. However, a majority of them, it seems, are not quite ready to be weaned entirely from those free flowing spigots. So they re-elected Clinton to keep the spigots open.

AUTHOR: Be that as it may, it isn't our purpose, here, to discuss particular legislative proposals except perhaps to illustrate a more primal idea that we may come up with.

Instead, let's start with some off-the-top-of-your-head remarks about what government is or what its purpose is. Or what it should be.

READER L: I'd say that it's a system devised to tax the earnings and property of the productive citizens among us and to transfer that money to unproductive and under-productive members of our society--and to that ever enlarging segment of the population employed by government.

READER B: It might be said that it's a system designed to protect the peace-loving members of society from the predators.

READER F (artist): It seems to me, that in a good bit of the world, the predators are in charge of government. The bullies all get together and lord it over the rest of the people. We call the head bully a dictator.

These authoritative types claim that the masses are incapable of governing themselves, or of managing their own lives, or of selecting their leaders. Putting on the mantle of divine right, they rule through intimidation and the use of violence. And what the authoritarian elitists take at the point of a gun, democratically elected elitists gain by playing on our fears and insecurities and by skillful use of various other manipulative devices--all in the pursuit of power.

READER G (reporter): I think you're right. What is it with these people? Down through the ages, from the pharaohs of Egypt, to Alexander the Great, to the emperors of Rome, Attila the Hun, Ghengis Khan, the Russian czars, Stalin, Hitler, Saddam Hussein--they never seem to have enough power. Why is that? What's driving them?

READER L: Let's not forget our very own, democratically elected power seekers. First, there was the grand-daddy of big government, in the USA, Franklin Delano Roosevelt. He gave the American people a "new deal." Unfortunately, the deck was stacked in favor of socialism. And then came Hubert Horatio Humphrey and Lyndon Baines Johnson, author and producer, respectively, of the "Great Society."

READER A: And now we have the next nominees for the Big Government Hall of Fame: William and Hilary Rodham Clinton. Despite President Clinton's statement that the era of big government is over, if they get their way, their claim to fame will be that they were the first in the USA. to take away more from the people, in taxes, than they're allowed to keep for themselves.

READER L: As to what's driving these people, they may say and they may believe that they care about people and are only doing what is right and necessary for the good of the nation.

But, in reality, it's fear that drives them. They are social cowards. Neurotics. Afraid to compete in a free, give and take society. The only way they can get along with people is to control them. And they never feel secure. As soon as they get one area or one group of people under control, they start worrying about the next.

READER G: How did they get that way?

READER D (couch potato): I can answer that. It's a matter of emotional immaturity--they never grew up. Specifically, they're suffering from what I call the <u>arrested two year old syndrome</u>.

READER G: What's that?

READER D: I'll tell you. This applies to bullies and all other control freaks. The list includes dictators, tyrants, socialists, all lovers of big government. And it might include one's boss, religious leader, spouse, parent, or anyone, for that matter.

As you, probably know, when a child reaches the age of around two, he enters a stage in his development where he becomes curious about his environment. He begins to test it's limits and to push against its boundaries, and to see what he can get away with and what he cannot. When he meets resistance, there are two ways he can respond in order to get what he wants. He can try being cute, clever and adorable. If that doesn't work, he resorts to kicking and screaming.

If you are a good, loving parent, you will let him explore and push to a point. But when he goes too far, you must let him know, somehow, that he's reached a limit. Anyway, most kids get through this stage learning there are limits to their behavior. And they grow up to be viable, law-abiding citizens. But if a child has little or no parental control or guidance, during this period, or if his parents stifle him with too much control or with control that is too harsh, he may develop into a bully--a grown up holy-terror. Or, depending on his glandular make-up, he may become a precocious, manipulative con-man.

And, as Reader L said, the fear of losing control drives such a person to increase and expand his control.

READER C (aerobics instruction): How do we get rid of dictators? How do we stop would-be dictators from getting control?

READER L: As I said, dictators are bullies, and the only way to deal with a bully is to carry a bigger stick and have the will and the skill to use it. For a country to get rid of a dictator, it usually requires outside help, either in the form of arms and supplies, or by an invading force. Preventing would-be dictators from ever taking over requires that we reject candidates who promise to do for us what we as families and individuals should do for ourselves, and requires that freedom loving citizens be ready, willing, and able to resist force with force.

We must have faith that the good people outnumber the bad people-- and, if sufficiently armed and motivated, the good guys will prevail over the bad guys.

READER G: How do we, in a democracy, guard against being conned by and controlled by big brother, big government, types? How can we get rid of the ones we have?

READER L: Simple. If an office seeker or office holder promises to take money from somebody else and transfer it to you, either as a grant, an entitlement, a free service, or a subsidy, vote against him. He's trying to get you to trade your soul for money and goodies.

READER D: It might help our understanding of the subject if we speculate on how and why government got started in the first place. What is known about that?

READER B: The first type of government was probably tribal in nature. The overall purpose was for the protection and welfare of the tribe. Presumably, the strongest, the bravest, the wisest, and most responsible member of the tribe became chief. Or maybe it was the biggest bully.

READER A: I understand the part about the protection of the tribe. But how about the welfare thing?

READER B: Well, that would have to do with passing on the knowledge of the elders to the young people. The knowledge of how to survive in the jungle, how to hunt and gather food, how to make weapons, tools, shelter and so forth. It would also involve resolving disputes between tribe members. And with establishing traditions and ceremonies, to promote a sense of unity and loyalty to the tribe and to one another.

READER G: I wonder what kind of punishment they dished out to wrongdoers.

READER B: An early form of punishment was stoning-- throwing rocks at the guilty party. Other forms were mutilation and burning at the stake. Also, there was banishment from the tribe. Today's equivalent of that is incarceration in jails and prisons.

READER A: The difference is that, back then, the banished tribesman had to hack it on his own, in the jungle. Today, we feed, clothe, and shelter them and give them free medical care.

READER G: Getting back to the welfare of the tribe. Is the passing on of knowledge and wisdom to the young necessarily the duty of the government?

READER B: In the beginning, the young people, more than likely, picked up knowledge along the way from parents or from other members of the tribe. If someone came up with some new idea or new bit of valuable information, or a new way of doing something, he or she might have been asked to go around and share it with others.

This, perhaps, brought about the concept of teaching and, eventually, the establishing of schools and universities.

READER D: The way government got involved might be illustrated by what the early settlers in our country did. The citizens would get together and build a school house, then, pass

39

the hat around for money to hire a teacher. Later on passing the hat evolved into a school tax.

READER A: So that's how taxation got started. Whoever thought it up should have been done away with, on the spot. I think we ought to go back to voluntary contributions to help the needy. And free enterprise should take care of nearly all the services now being provided by the government. I'd bet that we would have much better service for a lot less cost.

Also, government employees, whether elected officials or bureaucrats, should receive very low pay--about the same amount that people serving on juries get. Let's make government service an occasional or periodic duty, not a career.

READER B: Virtually dismantle the government--is that what you're saying?

READER A: I'd call it whittling down. Especially the federal government. That reminds me--back during the 1980 presidential campaign, I heard a radio newsman quoting one of the candidates. To many people, what the candidate said might have sounded like standard campaign fodder. But to me it was the revelation of a great truth. It got my attention and reverberated through me with the same intensity as the striking of a Chinese gong.

I could hardly wait for the evening news, to see how the statement would be debated among the pundits, the politicians, and on the editorial pages. But I never heard another word about it. Not one single word of response to what is possibly the greatest political, social, or philosophic statement ever made, having to do with the functioning of society.

READER B: What was the statement? Can you recall the exact words?

READER A: Verbatim. All twelve words. They were immediately engraved on my brain. For the life of me, I can't understand how it could have been over looked and ignored the way it was. With no comment. No debate. Nothing.

READER B: Okay. What was the statement?

READER A: Well, it was made by Ronald Reagan, in a 1980 campaign speech. Listen closely, now. And I'll bet you, too, will be able to repeat it word for word. I quote:

"All problems should be solved at the lowest level of responsibility possible."

READER D: "All problems should be solved at the lowest level of responsibility possible." I like it. On the surface, it's a nice, mild-mannered statement. But, oh, the profundity!

READER L: I would say it's seminal. Every facet of society could benefit by the employment of this idea.

AUTHOR: How can we apply this to government and to the betterment of society? How do we propagate the idea?

READER A: Here's the situation. You cannot have a great society unless you have great people. You cannot have a responsible, self-reliant, creative, morally upright nation without an overwhelming preponderance of responsible, self-reliant, creative, morally upright individuals.

How do we achieve this? First we must elect a government that will stop creating laws and programs that tend to weaken individual responsibility. And stop putting judges on the bench who relieve criminals of the responsibility of paying for their crimes.

Then, we must begin the process of shifting responsibility from the federal government back to the states; from the states back to local government; from local government back to the private sector --to businesses, unions, churches, foundations, and other charitable and cultural organization--and on down to families and individuals.

READER B: How do we decide at what level a particular problem should be dealt with?

READER L: I was just wondering about that, myself. I suppose that if you're looking at a particular problem--one that is now being handled at a high level of government--first, ask yourself this question: Is the problem being reduced or is the government making it worse? Welfare, for example.

READER A: Another thing. How much does it cost, compared to the same or similar problems that are being dealt with in the private sector or at a lower level of government?

READER D: Just think. Harry Truman was the cause of our depending on Washington to solve all our problems.

AUTHOR: Harry Truman? In what way?

READER D: Well, he had a sign on his desk which read: The Buck Stops Here. So, that's when everyone started shifting responsibility for their problems up the line. I think it's about time to start passing the buck back the other way.

READER B: I believe the tide is beginning to turn, already. Of course, the federal government is still mandating new programs, but the states have to come up with the bucks to pay for them. It won't be long before the states rebel against that.

READER G: There are some things in which all levels of society need to be involved. The most obvious is dealing with crime. Government alone cannot begin to solve this problem. The police cannot prevent every crime or catch every criminal. The reduction of crime requires that citizens take preventive and protective measures in cooperation with the police department. The more input and awareness there is from individuals, the less will be needed from the police. Everyone has got to understand that.

READER C: Are you saying that citizens should arm themselves and take lessons in gun use and other police techniques?

READER G: If awareness, alarm systems, locks, and other preventive measures don't get the job done, what other recourse is there?

READER C: At present? Perhaps none. But in the long term, we've got to reconstitute the family and revive the idea of character, of morality, self-reliance, and responsibility.

READER L: How right you are.

READER B: Getting back to former president Reagan's statement. In a way, it's related, somewhat, to the words of Thomas Jefferson: "The best governed are the least governed." The implication being that if individuals learn to control their own behavior and act civilly to each other, there will be less need for government.

READER E (young religious woman): What we need to be reminded of is that no matter how intelligent, responsible, courageous, well intentioned, and wise our government leaders might be, there is still a higher intelligence, a higher power, an infallible source of wisdom and strength, creativity and joy that is available to us through faith and prayer.

Moral behavior, love, and charity are of the spirit, one soul relating to another and with God.

READER L: I'll say amen to that. When we begin to let government replace God, we wind up with something like the late Soviet Union: a bored, dysfunctional society, in a state of spiritual, moral, and physical atrophy.

READER C: I suppose we all agree that the prime duty of the government is to protect our God given rights and to protect us against harm and unfair treatment, either from outside forces or from each other, and to adjudicate conflicts and disagreements. But what about the function that has to do with appropriating land and securing right-of-ways for parks, roads, government buildings and facilities?

And how about the category of government services, dealing with education, recreation, garbage collection, street maintenance, and the like?

And welfare--for those families and individuals who, for one reason or another, are unable to take care of themselves?

It may not be necessary for government to be involved in all of these things, but isn't it the duty of a civilized society to perform them? Especially, to care for those who cannot care or provide for themselves?

READER L: A very good question. The answer is yes. But not necessarily by government. There are many institutions that have been created for the care and enrichment of society. Government is only one among many--and it's probably the most wasteful and inefficient.

The greatest service a government can provide its citizens is to secure their freedom and protect their God-given rights.. Freedom to develop their own lives as they see fit--as long as they don't infringe on someone else's freedom. And freedom to join with others to pursue desired goals and to support worthwhile institutions and endeavors. To govern is to control, to coerce, and to determine. Now, good citizens in a society don't mind the government being involved in controlling criminals. And they don't mind being regimented and taxed to deal with an invading army. But they do seem to resent government forcing them to be charitable, or coercing them to support certain cultural endeavors. They'd rather have the freedom to choose, themselves, how much and to whom they would like to contribute. When the government gets into the charity business, the recipients begin to think of it as a right. And more and more people decide that they need to exercise that right and partake of that largesse.

But, when a person receives help from volunteer contributors, he is aware that it's not a right, but a gift from someone who deems the recipient worthy of support--someone who might be more interested than the government, in helping him to improve himself and become a productive citizen.

Society should strive to provide everyone with the opportunity for gainful employment. But government should not be in the business of providing everyone with a job. If everyone is guaranteed a job, there's no incentive to do it well. And, eventually, the job holder will begin to hate his job and to feel like a slave. That's why socialism will always fail.

We must have the right to succeed or fail on our own merits and to suffer when we fail. This builds character. Whereas, socialism and authoritative government stifles the development of character and destroys the spirit.

AUTHOR: Speaking of authoritative government, aren't all governments authoritative, to a certain extent?

READER L: I was alluding to dictatorship or oligarchy, where all the power is in either one person or a few people.

AUTHOR: That suggests that the broader the base of authority, the better the government. If so, then, is pure democracy the best form of government?

READER L: Not exactly: Majority rule can be just as tyrannical or destructive to a society as autocracy or oligarchy.

READER E (young religious woman): The ultimate authority is God. Our laws should reflect the will of God. Our lawmakers and administrators of the law should be selected according to their belief in that higher authority and that, as our founding fathers believed, all persons are equal in the sight of God and should be equal under the law.

AUTHOR: I suppose that we all agree that a government of laws is better than one that operates at the fancy of a dictator or oligarchy, or on the momentary whim of a majority of the citizens. And that the prime ingredient in a good system is its constitution--the foundation and framework upon which civilized government is built.

We in the United States should feel quite pleased with our constitution and our system of government. It isn't a pure democracy and it isn't exactly Plato's republic. How should it be characterized?

READER G: I would describe it as being a democratically elected representative type constitutional republic, with three equal branches: legislative, administrative, and judicial.

READER A: You forgot about the biggest branch of all--The bureaucracy.

READER L: That's not a branch--the bureaucracy is a cancer. A malignant cancer. And if we don't change direction, soon, we'll wind up like people in the former Soviet Union.

AUTHOR: Who is responsible for this societal malignancy? Is it our government leaders? Could it be we have a flawed constitution? Should we blame the employees of the government? The people on welfare? Other recipients of government largesse?

READER A: There's nothing wrong with the system. It's just being misused. Who's to blame? I don't think we should necessarily blame the politicians and the bureaucrats--they're just practicing their own brand of entrepreneurship. And don't blame the people on welfare and the government grant leeches--they're just doing their thing too.

READER G: Other than criminals, that leaves only us--the gainfully employed, law-abiding, taxpayers.

READER A: Right! When are we going to put our collective foot down and quit feeding this monster? Aren't we still the majority? Can't we get together and elect candidates in all levels of government who believe, as Ronald Reagan does, that if government would only get off the backs of the citizens and get its hands out of their pockets, the American people are quite capable of managing their own lives and of building a happy and productive society?

READER L: Mr. Reagan also believes, as did our founding fathers, that the best thing a government can do is to secure the liberty and freedom of every worthy citizen.

READER B: Excuse me. Haven't you just posed a paradox?

READER L: How so?

READER B: Well, earlier, you said that to govern is to control. How can you rectify that with saying the government should provide the people with liberty and freedom?

READER L: The rectifying ingredient is the adjective "worthy". Government secures the liberty and freedom of WORTHY citizens by CONTROLLING the actions of predatory citizens and by defending against foreign predators.

I believe as Mr. Reagan does, and as the founding fathers did, that free people create a livelier, more prosperous, and more desirable society than enslaved citizens can ever hope to.

And thousands of people around the world that are seeking to come to America, apparently believe it also.

READER G: Speaking of liberty and freedom, I read, the other day, that only about one person in five, on this planet, live under a government that even comes close to guaranteeing its citizens the individual rights we enjoy. One in five.

AUTHOR: That is a depressing statistic.

READER L: More depressing to me is the growing number of Americans with so little faith in their own abilities that they are willing to trade liberty for the promise of life long, comprehensive security. Cradle to the grave. Womb to the tomb. And as they reach out for this dangled carrot, they seem not to be aware of the sound of shackles being snapped shut. Or the click of prison doors being closed. Or the clouding of the mind and dimming of the spirit.

To those who still cherish freedom, here's something to think about. It's a quote from newspaper columnist Dorothy Thompson: "When liberty is taken from us by force it can be restored by force. When it is relinquished voluntarily by default it can never be recovered."

Chapter 7

READER C {female aerobics instructor}: It's a funny thing. In chapter six, we concluded that the prime requisite of a good society is a government that protects the freedom and the God - given rights of the citizens--but that the less government there is, the better the society.

READER L {business man}: I think what we agreed on was that the better the society, the less need there is for government.

READER C: Okay. Let's discuss the criteria for a good society. What is it that we need more of in order to lessen the need for government?

AUTHOR: I suppose we should start with the everyday needs and concerns of the average citizen: food, clothing, shelter, transportation, healthcare, recreation, the arts, religion, crime control, education, clean environment. It's sometimes referred to as quality of life.

READER D {couch potato}: It might be that the simplest and best way to approach this subject is to pick out from all the different societies around the world the one we think is the best-- then dissect it, analyze it, and discuss the various elements and dynamics of it.

READER G {reporter}: There's an organization that, once a year, comes up with a list of the most livable cities in the USA. They use a number of criteria, such as low crime, cost of living, quality of services, cultural aspects, and so forth, to make their determination.

It might be a good thing if some such group could come up, once a year, with a list of the world's best societies. Or maybe once every four years--an Olympic Societal Excellence Competition, so to speak.

READER B {professor}: That's a fascinating proposition. But it's chock-full of complication. First, how do we determine what constitutes a given society? Some societies may spill across national boundaries. and some nations contain several or parts of several different societies.

AUTHOR: Well, let's don't get too technical here--or too intellectual. Let's just say we're looking for the best place on Earth to live.

There's two ways we can proceed. We can come up with a set of criteria for a good society. Then, try to find out what place on Earth comes closest to fitting the criteria.

The other approach is to pick a place that has the reputation for being the nearest thing to Paradise. And then study its elements and seek to find out what makes it tick.

READER K {retired farmer}: Bingo! I think I have a nominee. During World War Two, I was stationed, for ten months, on the island of Upolu, in Western Samoa. When it comes to a happy, peaceful, and well run society, this one would be hard to beat, if it's still the same as it was back then. What little amount of government they had was mostly in Apia, the capitol. Western Samoa, at that time, was a protectorate of New Zealand.

Out in the villages, you wouldn't be much aware of anything resembling an official of the government. Just about everything was handled at the family level. A family group in a village was usually an extended family--a small clan--headed by a matai, or patriarch. One of his duties was parceling out the family farm land to different family units.

READER A {insurance man}: In what way, specifically, was it a good society?

READER K: Well, as I said, nearly everything was handled at the family level. Responsibility started early in life, around age five. The young boys, upon reaching that age, learned from the older boys, starting with fishing, climbing coconut trees and, later on, canoe making and Samoan style carpentry.

At that age, a young girl's first responsibility was to look after her younger siblings. As she grew older, she took on newer responsibilities, such as household duties, mat weaving, gathering bark for making tapa cloth, and farm work, while still keeping an eye on younger children. Each group passed on what it knew to those younger and learned new skills from the next older group.

50

READER L {business man}: Seems to me that was a prime example of things being handled at the lowest level of responsibility. How did this way of doing things affect the quality of life?

READER K: Well, as anthropologist, Margaret Mead reported, there was virtually no crime--none that I was aware of--no hunger, no mental or emotional problems. I never encountered anyone who was up-tight. Everyone seemed to have a good sense of humor. There was a lot of good natured kidding.

The most popular native song was *File' Mu*, which means take it easy.

READER B: According to the book "Coming of Age In Samoa", by Miss Mead, Samoans are a bit casual when it comes to sex, with sexual experimentation and liaisons starting not very long after the beginning of puberty.

READER K: That wasn't the impression I had. I made friends with a Samoan who worked at our camp. His name was Tunu. If I remember correctly, he said that it was the custom that boys and girls were kept apart, starting at a very early age and that it was taboo to look at or talk to each other until they were twenty-one years old.

A couple of months ago, I read that Margaret Mead's reports on the sexual habits of Samoans have been discounted by other anthropologists. I don't remember if there was a connection, but the item mentioned something about her being a lesbian.

Anyway, that prompted me to check out her book from the library. According to the book, even though they didn't use birth control devices, it was very rare that any of this casual sex--"Under the palms", as she put it--ever resulted in pregnancy. It was almost exclusively the married women that had babies. That seems a bit contradictory to me.

READER D: What did they do after coming of age? When you were there, did it appear to be a free-love society?

READER K: Well, I didn't delve into the matter that much. If I had known that, fifty years later, I'd be having this conversation, I would have studied the situation more and taken notes.

In Apia, the capitol, where there were quite a few New Zealand government personnel, Europeans, and mixed race people and some westernized Samoans, the situation was more or less like any other port city.

I was in the regimental band--I played the trombone. And I remember that a couple of boys in the band had intimate girl friends in Apia. One of the guys ran into a little trouble with his Samoan sweetheart. She accused him of infecting her with a "cold"--the venereal kind. He claimed he had gotten it from her.

I don't recall anyone fraternizing with any of the nearby village girls. The closest I came to that happened one afternoon at the edge of our camp. Some fat old woman from Apia had come there with an old-fashioned crank operated ice cream freezer and was selling ice cream to the marines.

I was leaning against a tree, looking around, and I saw this beautiful, golden skinned half-caste young lady, with honey colored hair, come walking down the little road that led from the banana plantation.

I smiled at her and she smiled back and came up to me. Then, she reached up and put her hand on top of my head and said, "Malingi {marine} tall." She was wearing a lava lava { a large piece of cloth wrapped around her body from the waist down} and a light colored shirt. Adding to the cautious excitement I felt, at this encounter, was the machete that dangled from her hip.

She spoke English fairly well and we talked a bit. Finally, I asked her if I could come down to her village and visit her, sometime. She said okay. I asked her how I'd go about finding her. She told me she lived in the missionary's house. I never got around to looking her up.

READER G: Getting back to the fact, as Margaret Mead wrote, very few unmarried girls got pregnant, perhaps the alleged liaisons, "under the palms," were innocent, platonic affairs. Maybe the opiate tropical splendor, the balmy trade-wind breezes, and dark limped eyes glistening in the moonlight was pleasure enough. Maybe they have a low threshold for arousal of the brain's euphoria center. And, according to Reader

F and that little mouse, back in chapter two, that's better than sex.

READER K: You may have a point. There seems to be a prevailing air of dreamy enchantment about the place.

READER A {insurance man}: Or maybe the sex activity they engaged in fell somewhere short of intercourse.

READER K: That's a possible explanation. In fact, there was a parody of the song, "Lovely Hula Hands", that we picked up from the natives. The first line went like this: "Lovely hula hands--fu fu in the sand."

AUTHOR: From the conversation, thus far, it appears that, in this ideal society, the main occupation had to do with raising and gathering food and that just about every member of the society-men, women, and children--participated in it.

READER K: That's true. About the only specialized occupation was fale' building. Fale'--rhymes with holly--is Samoan for house. This work was done by certain men skilled in the art. The fales were built without nails. Everything was tied together. There were no walls--just posts and a thatch roof, made from palm fronds. They hung woven blinds to keep out the sun and rain.

Both sexes wove mats. And both participated in the cooking of the food, which consisted mostly of fruits and vegetables, bread fruit and taro root, fish and a little bit of pork.

There wasn't much furniture, other than mats and baskets. And very little in the way of possessions, except for wooden bowls and a few pots and pans, musical instruments, and primitive jewelry.

READER B: What kind of education system did they have?

READER K: Well, I know they had missionary schools and, perhaps, government schools. Nearly all the citizens could read, write, and speak both English and Samoan.

According to Margaret Mead, being a high achiever in Samoa was something that was frowned upon, impolite, and an insult to the rest of the tribe. There was one exception--dancing. When it comes to Siva dancing, which was mostly solo dancing, you could be as spirited, as creative, and technically advanced as you cared to be. And you would be roundly applauded for a good performance.

READER E: What kind of religion did they practice?

READER K: Christianity. Nearly every village had a church--usually staffed by missionaries and sometimes by Samoans. There were vestiges of Samoan religious practice. For instance, instead of saying grace, they would pick up food with their fingers and kiss it before eating it.

According to Margaret Mead, the Samoans accepted Christianity, as well as European ideas of law and order, in a perfunctory sort of way. And some of them had become teachers, nurses, policemen, and ministers or priests in the village churches. But most of the everyday living, dressing, and way of doing things went on in the traditional manner.

The New Zealand government, respecting their ways, usually appointed the highest ranking matai in a village to be the official government head at the village.

One of the few laws imposed on the natives was to stop the practice of beating promiscuous or adulterous females. They continued to cut off all their hair, however. One of the things the missionaries succeeded in doing was persuading the females to cover their breasts.

About the only things the Samoans accepted willingly from the Europeans were steel knives, axes, and so forth. Also, medical treatment--especially for mumu {filariasis} and skin diseases such as yaws.

READER B: From what you say, it seems that the Samoans, at that time, were quite confident with their easygoing way of life and were in no hurry to emulate modern, progressive, frenetic, complicated, <u>civilized</u> societies.

READER K: Correct. And, as to their acceptance of steel hand tools--it's quite understandable. Those tools afforded them more time to take it easy.

READER B: Some primitive societies, when confronted with civilization, just seem to accept it as superior to their way of life and try to emulate it and let their own culture disintegrate. Other groups flee deeper into the jungle or into the desert--and want nothing to do with civilization.

READER K: The way I see it, the Samoans are highly advanced when it comes to understanding human nature. I suppose that's why Robert Louis Stevenson loved the place and the people so much--and why he made his home there, at Vailima, and was buried there. The Samoans have a very good sense of humor and seem to have a better understanding of what constitutes the good life.

READER A: So--a good life is one with no furniture and practically no factory made goods, no walls, no plumbing, no electricity, no cars, telephones or television. Nothing much except raw nature, a little primitive music and dancing, and each other.

I don't think that would go over very well here. In this climate, we couldn't survive without furnaces, air conditioning, machinery, cars, tractors, and all that kind of stuff.

READER K: How about the American Indians? The Eskimos? How did they survive? How about our ancestors? In fact, you could take a look at my family, back during the Great Depression, and you wouldn't find a great deal of difference between how we lived and how the Samoans lived. I was six years old when the depression of the 1930's came along. We were living in town at the time. My father, who had left the farm to become a carpenter, wasn't getting much work, so he decided to take up farming again. We moved out to a share-cropper farm. Being a share-cropper meant that we had to give the man who owned the land one-third of what we made on the farm.

Anyway, we were lucky at that. Even though we had no electricity, no running water or indoor plumbing, no refrigeration, we fared better than a lot of city people.

Like the Samoans, we lived almost entirely off the land: water from a spring, food from the fields, fuel from chopped down trees. Like Samoan children, we started working and having responsibilities at a very young age.

And our extended-family relationships were similar, in many ways, to that of the Samoans. Since we had no such thing as television and, for a long time, not even radio, we entertained each other. Relatives came to visit occasionally. The grown-ups recounted old family stories and experiences. We younger people--siblings, cousins, and neighbor kids--played folk games, posed riddles, told ghost stories, or went out exploring the countryside.

Like Samoans, we were very close to nature and aware of its beauty and wonder--and its ever changing moods. Back then, there was no pollution that we were aware of. The rivers and creeks were clean. The air was clear. There was not much noise--the sounds you heard were nature sounds.

That's all changed, now. Farming has changed. It's become highly mechanized, specialized, subsidized, and electrified--and boring. Before, farmers grew a little bit of everything: cotton, corn, hay, grains, fruit and vegetables, and they raised cattle, pigs, sheep, and chickens. Today, you have to specialize in order to compete. One farmer may specialize in soy beans. Another will raise beef cattle. Another hay and grains. Some just grow pine trees for the paper mill. And now there are poultry farms, dairy farms, apple growers, peanut farmers, and so forth.

Family farmers are selling out to corporate farms. Nowadays, it's all big business and high-tech, involving large capitol outlays. With all the mechanization that has taken place, the percentage of the population engaged in farming, in the USA, has dropped from 17.8 per cent, in 1940, to under two per cent, today. That is 2 per cent farmers and 98 percent everything else.

In Samoa, at the time I was there, it was more like 98 per cent farming and 2 per cent everything else.

I'm not sure my brothers and sisters would agree with me-- but I suspect they might--that life on the farm, as we experienced it in the 1930's, was more enjoyable and more meaningful than anything we've tried since, or anything going on, now, in this high-tech, high stress, over crowded, polluted world we live in today.

I feel sorry for anyone who didn't grow up on a farm. Nowadays, that's just about everyone.

AUTHOR: I'm wondering if, as you say, growing up on a small family farm and making a living from the land is the best life there is--the happiest and most meaningful--then what is the opposite? What is the worst way?

READER K: I suppose it would be living on welfare in an inner-city slum, in a polluted, hopeless, crime-ridden environment.

READER L {business man}: If that's the case, perhaps the solution to the welfare mess is to require all people on welfare to move out to a farm. It might not have much effect on the adults, but the process of planting seeds, waiting for them to sprout, and then nurturing the young plants and protecting them from being overcome by weeds or insects, until maturity, and then harvesting the fruits of one's labor could make a profound impression on the youngsters--powerful enough, perhaps, to enable them to break away from the dehumanizing welfare system.

AUTHOR: Sounds logical to me. In fact, recently, I read something about a small program that's been started in New York City where a piece of land has been divided into garden plots and assigned to families from inner-city areas.

READER D: Some such program might also help solve the crime problem. How about if we make convicted criminals serve their time on a 1930's style farm. However, to me that would be cruel and unusual punishment.

READER K: In a way, that's been tried, too. Just this morning, on television, there was a report about criminals living and working on a horse ranch, in a rehabilitation program. According to the report, the results, so far, are quite promising. The program has to do with breaking in and training horses. Reference was made to the fact that the horse and the criminal, to begin with, are both free spirits--wild and untamed. During the process, they learn from each other. I suppose what they learn is, that to get along in this world and to receive the benefits available in a civilized society, you have to be reined in a bit, so to speak, and submit to a certain amount of discipline.

READER B: Getting back to the Samoans, were they not, at one time, a warlike society?

READER K: That is correct. They used to go about in large outrigger canoes, traveling hundreds of miles across open water to do their fighting.

READER B : If that is true, then might we assume that European and American influences had more than a little to do with Samoan society becoming a peaceful and orderly one?

READER K: You may have a point.

READER B: Shouldn't we then at least consider the possibility that New Zealand, trustee of Western Samoa, and the United States, trustee of American Samoa, might be even better societies than Samoan society.?

READER K: It's certainly something to think about. However, it could be that Samoan society, which was pretty good to begin with, has become even better by accepting certain refinements from European and American cultures. Incidentally, in 1962, Western Samoa became an independent republic.

READER L: New Zealand might well be a contender for the title of <u>Best Place to Live</u>, especially, now, that they are in the process of dismantling their experiment with socialism. If Samoan life is a little too primitive for your taste, and you're looking for a society having the stability of Samoa but with a more elaborate culture, New Zealand just might be the place.

READER G: Before we leave beautiful, romantic Samoa, perhaps we should describe more fully its economic system. Is it capitalism, socialism? Or is it too primitive to even call a system?

READER L: From what Reader K has related, I'd say it's based on the concept of family property rights--chiefly the ownership of land. As older members of the family die off, their piece of the family land is turned over to younger adult members. It's not primitive.

Primitive societies look on the land as belonging to itself and it's theirs to use, on a temporary basis, until they decide to move on or until they are driven off. Or, they might look upon it as belonging to the tribe.

AUTHOR: Speaking of owning land, I suppose we'd all like to have a piece of land to call our own--even though very few of us would care to make our living as farmers.

READER A: You can't say that any individual owns land in the United States. We just rent it from the government.

AUTHOR: What do you mean by that?

READER A: We pay rent in the form of property tax. Stop paying it and you'll find out what I mean. Also, if I'm really the owner of a piece of property, how come the government can run a highway through it, against my wishes?

READER B: Let's get back to the proposal to move welfare families out to the farm. Wouldn't this involve some kind of land redistribution--taking land from large landowners and redistributing it to non-owners?

READER K: Nah--at least not right away. We're not talking about large numbers of new people becoming farmers. As I said, earlier, less than two per cent of Americans are farmers and, yet, they produce enough food to feed the U.S. with enough left over to help feed a good bit of the rest of the world. That's not going to change much.

The main thing is to get the teenage or young adult welfare parent--or parents--with babies or young children away from the high crime, drug ridden slums, and out into the country. And have them live there long enough to learn something more meaningful than taking or selling dope, robbing, mugging, or shooting people--or being robbed, mugged, or shot.

There could be a number of ways that program might be set up. But I think every program should require that each family would have the use of a small piece of land for a garden of their own, where the whole family can participate in planting and cultivating this family enterprise and, as Reader L said, in harvesting the fruits of their labor.

This undertaking would be mainly for the benefit of the young, teaching them how to relate to their environment in a meaningful way--and how to gain confidence by accomplishing something worthwhile.

READER D : Just think, if Barry Goldwater had been elected president, in 1964, we wouldn't be having all these welfare worries, or rampant crime and drug problems.

READER B: What do you mean by that?

READER D: Remember? Didn't the Democrats, during the campaign, say if we elected Mr. Goldwater, he would take us back to 1864? I'd say about half the people, in 1864, lived on farms, crime was much less than today, and horses produced fertilizer--not carbon monoxide.

READER C: Well, Mr. Goldwater was not elected. And this is the mid-nineteen nineties, and we are faced with serious problems--crime, pollution, inner-city misery, and the breakdown of the family. Also, the world is getting too crowded. I heard, recently, that if the present rate of increase is maintained, the world population will pass twenty billion by the year 2050. A four hundred percent increase.

READER B: To put it another way, at that rate, the population density of the world would go from around 90 persons per square mile of land, today, to nearly 400 in 2050.

The U.S. would go from 70 persons per square mile, to 280 per square mile--making us slightly more crowded than European countries are now.

READER C: If the population does quadruple, there will have to be wholesale life-style changes or we'll all die of pollution.

READER K: It could be that, by then, we will run out of things that cause pollution. Fossil fuels, for instance. Anyway, what we really need to do is reduce the population. Cut it in half. That would leave 45 persons per square mile; that works out to thirteen acres per person--or 52 acres for a family of four.

I think we ought to do away with big cities, big industry, big everything. Do the people who reside in New York, Chicago, and Los Angeles--with all that smog, noise pollution, and people jammed up against each other, and millions of cars fuming up the place--really enjoy living there?

Do they really like the kind of jobs they have? How meaningful can it be to work in a factory, doing one little thing over and over, or to be a garbage man, or a stockbroker, a supermarket checker or an insurance salesman?

READER A: Hey! Don't knock the insurance business- -we provide a very meaningful service--financial security and peace of mind. I might add that if we turn millions of people into farmers, they're going to need crop insurance, what with all the floods, droughts, and insect plagues that come along.

READER L: I doubt if there will be a big rush of people moving out to the farm, anytime soon. To Reader K, growing things on the farm, raising animals, and being close to nature is perhaps the most meaningful and satisfying thing imaginable. But to a third generation welfare recipient, having to depend on his own efforts and the vagaries of nature for his subsistence could cause him considerable anxiety.

About the only thing meaningful to some welfare recipients is that monthly check, food stamps, and all the other entitlements they receive, courtesy of the taxpayers.

READER B: If we look back to our own history, we'll find that a substantial number of people who came to settle this country were from the lower rungs of European society. Many of them came straight from prisons and from city slums.

This was particularly true of the colony that set up in Savannah. James Oglethorpe, with a private charter from the British government, brought people here hoping to improve their miserable lives by helping them to become self-subsistent. Oglethorpe and his twenty partners also hoped to start a lucrative silk industry.

For the first few years, the colonists couldn't even grow enough food to feed themselves. They claimed it was too hot to work in the fields. Supplementary food had to be brought in from Charleston. Oglethorpe and his partners were disappointed with the results of their endeavor {the silk making project was a failure} and they turned the colony back over to the British government, one year before their charter expired.

Eventually, however, the people adjusted to the climate and to their new environment and the colony began to thrive.

This pioneering process has been repeated many times, since. And, with a bit of updating and a few adjustments, the basic idea of helping society's misfits, by transplanting them to a new environment, is, I think, still a valid one. The big problem is that there is less and less space available.

READER C: How do we stop population growth or even reduce the number of people we have?

READER A: The solution, of course, is birth control. And there's two ways to pursue it--by government limitation, as

61

practiced in China, or by intense social pressure and persuasion, like that now being applied to cigarette smokers, here in the United States.

READER L: The best thing the government could do would be to stop subsidizing--and in effect encouraging--illegitimate births via its welfare policies.

READER G: In our discussion, it's been suggested that to better our society we need to simplify our life-style and reduce the size of the population--or at least to stop its growth. Is there no alternative?

Isn't it possible that by coming up with a clean way of producing energy--through improved solar cells or a breakthrough in the fusion process--and by recycling everything we use, and by finding substitutes for products that pollute--we could double or triple the world population and, at the same time, improve the environment and our quality of life?

READER B: It's possible. But only if we can get everyone thinking and working in that direction.

READER C: Twenty billion people achieving that kind of utopia is about as likely to happen as Reader D dancing the lead in Swan Lake. We ought to look toward holding it to the present 5.6 billion souls.

Most people around the world probably agree that we need to do something about population growth and about the drain on the earth's resources. Also, that we should be less wrapped up in material things and more involved in interpersonal and spiritual matters. But, when it comes to the local level, we seem to clamor for more industry, more acres of pavement, more cars, appliances, gadgets and--yes, more people--for our particular city or county. It's ridiculous.

READER F {artist}: Yeah, the chamber of commerce wants more industry because the new wage earners will spend more at chamber members' businesses. News papers see it bringing in more advertising. And local governments love the increased tax base and increased revenues flowing into their coffers.

There are some good things going on. Government, industry, business, along with individual citizens are working together on reducing pollution, on recycling and on preserving wet lands and wilderness areas.

And, even though we flock to the shopping malls and super stores for inexpensive, mass produced, plastic wrapped goods and pre-packaged food products, there has been, in the last thirty or forty years, a tremendous number of people that have taken up all sorts of handcrafts, such as pottery, wood working, needle work, and so forth. Art and craft festivals have sprung up all over the place. Nowadays, even an artist like me can make a living drawing and painting.

And there seems to be a growing number of do-it-yourself carpenters, plumbers, electricians and mechanics.

The reason for this, I believe, is that people feel a meaningful sense of accomplishment when they do these things-- a sense of being more in tune with their environment and with other people.

What I'm trying to get across is that we are quite capable of--even in a technically complex, highly mechanized, mass production type nation, such as ours--of developing into a better society. A society of responsible, self-reliant, adventurous, creative, diverse, friendly, tolerant, peace-loving citizens--and, like the Samoan society, with virtually no crime, hunger, or mental illness.

It's not that we all have to become subsistence farmers to achieve this. Or sleep on mats, or climb coconut trees. What makes the Samoan society so successful, no doubt, is the strong extended-family structure and the way they bring up their children to become responsible, well adjusted adults. Also, their closeness to nature and, very likely, their "take it easy" philosophy.

READER K: I think you've hit the nail on the head. In Samoa, if you get down on your luck, sick or disabled, you look to your extended family for help. In the U.S. we seek extended unemployment benefits, extended welfare assistance, and hundreds of other government goodies.

Another reason, perhaps, why young Samoans grow up to be well adjusted adults is because of the fact that the native huts have no walls. Kids grow up witnessing old people dying, babies being born, and just about everything adults do. They learn by osmosis.

READER D: If the huts have no walls, I suppose everybody knows everyone else's business. They don't need television. In the afternoon, instead of watching a soap opera, at 2:00 P.M., just watch what goes on in the hut to your right. Then, at 3:00 P.M., look at the one on the other side. For the six o'clock news, just take a stroll around the village. There's a thousand stories in the naked village. That's what I call real live entertainment.

READER C: The underlying lesson is not necessarily that we should live in houses without walls--but that perhaps we need to be more aware of each other. And that we should tear down walls of prejudice, intolerance, hostility, apathy and unconcern. And that we should become more neighborly and cooperative.

READER G: Question. Can we really say that a primitive society, anywhere, has any relevance to a highly advanced first-world nation, such as ours?

AUTHOR: Why not? This dialogue is about searching for primal knowledge. It seems to me that studying primitive society is a logical place to look for primal knowledge.

READER K: I agree. Especially Western Samoa. How did it go from a warlike primitive society, of a century or two ago, to the peaceful, highly functional semi-civilized society of fifty years ago? And what is it like today? Is it still a happy, easy-going society, virtually free of crime, mental illness, and illegitimacy? Or has it become sullied by contact with the rest of the world?

READER D: Well, why don't you take a little trip, west of Pago Pago, and see for yourself?

READER K: It's pronounced Pahngo Pahngo by the natives. But hey! That's a good idea--I would definitely like to see some more of Samoa.

Chapter 8

AUTHOR: I see in the newspaper that another attempt by some members of Congress to raise the tax on tobacco products has been defeated. Several years ago, the Clinton administration proposed a $12.50 per pound tax on tobacco products. That would have resulted in me having to pay more in taxes on a fourteen ounce can of Granger pipe tobacco than I'd pay for the tobacco.

That would have been an outrage. I don't know about cigarette smokers or tobacco chewers--but I think pipe smokers should be encouraged--not persecuted.

READER G: Why should they be encouraged?

AUTHOR: Well, one day several years ago, I heard on the radio that someone had taken a survey and discovered that pipe smokers, on average, live longer than nonsmokers.

To me that is an astounding and significant piece of news. Just think: pipe smokers live longer than nonsmokers! I fully expected to see a more detailed report in the evening paper or on the network news. But as yet I haven't seen or heard another word about it.

That's too bad. I would like to know why pipe smokers live longer. Is it because only healthy, stable, genetically enhanced people become pipe smokers? Or is it due to the fact that pipe smoking is an art and a discipline that requires a person to develop certain qualities in himself that are conducive to longevity? Qualities described with such words as deliberate, stable, contemplative, even tempered, etc.

READER G: Have you tried to contact any organization such as the Cancer Society or the Surgeon General's office?

AUTHOR: I've written to several such places. I even wrote Dear Abby. The only reply I ever receive is that pipe smoking may cause mouth cancer.

READER G: Why don't pipe smokers get lung cancer--like cigarette smokers do?

AUTHOR: Simple. Pipe smokers, as a rule don't inhale. Neither do cigar smokers.

READER G: Why do cigarette smokers inhale and why do pipe smokers not inhale?

AUTHOR: I may have an answer to that question. One Christmas my wife gave me a book called The Pipe Smoker, written by two psychologists and published by Harper and Row. One of the subjects dealt with the difference between cigarette smokers and pipe smokers. It seems that cigarette smokers are usually extroverts by nature. Extroverts, according to the authors, have a high threshold for cortex (higher brain) arousal and require more outside stimuli to excite the cortex. The inhaled nicotine is one source of stimulation.

On the other hand, most pipe smokers appear to be stable introverts. Introverts have a low cortex arousal threshold and are oftentimes over stimulated by whatever may be going on around them--sometimes to the point of stress. The deliberate routine of cleaning the pipe, filling the bowl with tobacco, lighting the pipe and puffing along at regular intervals tends to distract the pipe smoker from whatever may be causing him stress and allows him to relax. Any excess tension he may have felt, before, goes up in smoke once he lights his pipe. And since pipe smokers don't inhale there is very little, if any, effect from nicotine.

READER C (aerobics instructor): Why do you say pipe smoking is an art? It seems to me to be just a messy, smelly habit where the pipe smoker uses more matches than tobacco.

AUTHOR: The art in one respect, is in keeping the pipe lit without using so many matches. That's the criteria they use at pipe smoking contests.

READER G: How long have you been practicing the art?

AUTHOR: I took up pipe smoking when I was in the service, back during World War II. At first it was torture-- blistered tongue from drawing too hard or from using too many matches and frustration from not being able to sit back and enjoy it the way my buddy Leonard Riebel from Minnesota did. After awhile, with him as my mentor, I learned the techniques and self-control necessary to enjoy the art.

Eventually, years later, I was able to achieve pipe smokers nirvana, the ability to smoke a pipe all the way down to the dottle using not more than two matches. And occasionally I'm able to reach that super exalted plateau of having to use only one single solitary match.

READER D (couch potato): Wow! Only one match? Great achievement. Incidentally, why is it that it's generally men who smoke pipes? In fact, except for Lil' Abner's Mammy Yokum, I don't recall ever seeing a woman smoke a pipe.

AUTHOR: Let's keep it that way. Other than hunting, pipe smoking is about the only refuge left for male chauvinism.

READER C: Beside the fact that it's a filthy, smelly habit, one reason women don't smoke pipes is that it wastes a lot of time. Also, we're more considerate of those around us. Some people are allergic to tobacco fumes and can suffer an asthma attack from just a whiff or two.

READER G: What is the equivalent stress reliever for women--something they do that men don't usually do?

READER C: Probably knitting or crocheting. Not only is it relaxing, it's also creative and useful as well. I think smoking should be banned in all public buildings and even outdoors in crowded places. And it should be against the law to smoke around children, anywhere, anytime.

As for that other macho male indulgence, I cannot understand why anyone would want to go out and shoot living, breathing animals just for the sport of it.

READER L (businessman): Because it's primal. Our earliest ancestors were hunters. Incidentally, the fish and game commission needs to extend this year's deer hunting season. We're overpopulated with deer in this part of the state.

For your information, if it weren't for sportsmen and wildlife associations working with the government to control animal populations--thinning out some groups that have grown too large and working to increase the numbers in undersized groups-- many species of our furry and feathered friends might not still be around.

READER C: I know--but the problem is that in the cities we have all these guns, but there are no animals to shoot. So people start shooting each other. We even have children killing children.

READER L: Well, for that, I blame the perpetrators of the Great Society. Those paternalistic, big government programs are usurping the father's traditional role of providing for his family. And the huge tax revenues required to run these programs are making it harder for business and industry to provide enough jobs.

There's not much doubt that if every child could grow up having a responsible father around, a father who on occasion might take him hunting or fishing, juvenile crime would not be much of a problem.

READER A (insurance man): Great Society programs, however, are not the only problem. How about the woman's liberation movement?

The main goal of this movement is to make women equal to men. Why they would want to sink to that level, I don't know. Throughout history, it's been the gentler sex that has had a civilizing effect on the human race. They probably invented the institution of marriage.

But nowadays they are trying to be just like men. How can we respect them anymore? They're invading one male bastion after another. First it was the poolroom, then the barroom, the board room, the locker room, the battlefield, outer space, and now I hear they're demanding to be allowed to use the golf course on weekends. Where will it end?

Anyway, it's up to women to resurrect the family and bring civility and equilibrium back into society.

For things to get better, women must return to their true nature which I think has to do with nurturing and with the desire for a reliable, protective husband, happy healthy children, and a nice home in a secure community--and with inspiring men to rise above their own basic nature.

The way it works, the man proposes and the woman disposes. So, for the sake of the family and society in general, when a man tries to proposition a woman, she should keep saying no until he comes up with the right proposal--one that involves him joining her at the altar before she joins him in bed. And such a proposal should be accompanied with character references and proof of reliability.

AUTHOR: Excuse me. You've made some interesting points but I think they belong back in Chapter seven. This chapter is supposed to be about pipe smoking.

READER C: Tobacco and firearms are a menace to society. What else is left to be said?

AUTHOR: Whoa, Nellie. Once or twice a day I go outside to smoke my pipe. In the morning, I might watch the sun come up, listen to the birds, or look at squirrels running around in the trees while I enjoy my pipe. In the evening, I usually smoke in the back yard and watch the sun go down, listen to the crickets, see fireflies blink and the stars come out, and listen to the happy shouts of children playing up on Coral Avenue. In what way am I a menace to society? How much am I polluting the air, compared to the hundreds of cars going by on the street in front of my house?

Now, if I were to inhale, as cigarette smokers do, and smoke thirty or forty times a day, indoors, that might be a problem. There's a warning on every pack of cigarettes that says smoking cigarettes causes lung cancer. There's no such warning on pipe tobacco.

Now, they're saying second-hand smoke is dangerous. But I'm not fully convinced of that. If tobacco smoke is so harmful, how come George Burns, who smoked ten or twelve cigars a day, was still doing show business gigs at age ninety-eight?

READER H (musician): Another example of a long living, productive person was the late great cellist, Pablo Casals. He was a pipe smoker, and often smoked his pipe while practicing the cello. I'm not sure but I believe he lived into his nineties.

It might be that being a successful productive person--one who remains continually enthusiastic about his work and about life in general--has something to do with good health and longevity.

AUTHOR: Another thing, why is it that one person might say to me, when I'm smoking: "Oh, that smells so good--I just love the smell of burning pipe tobacco."

And then someone else might hold his or her nose and look daggers at me.

69

READER H: Could it be that the person who likes it is a happy, relaxed, positive type person and the person who doesn't is an uptight, dissatisfied, unhappy, hypochondriac?

AUTHOR: A very significant question.   Something psychologists ought to look into.

As to the report I heard on radio about pipe smokers living longer than nonsmokers, I think the Surgeon General should check it out.   And if it's true, require tobacco companies to put the following message on each can of tobacco: The Surgeon General has determined that pipe smokers live longer than nonsmokers.

Let's accentuate the positive for a change.

READER F (artist):   If this chapter is about pipe smoking, when are you going to tell us how to smoke a pipe full of tobacco, using not more than two matches?   In all the years I've smoked a pipe, I don't think I've accomplished that feat more than a couple of times.   In fact, I often find pipe smoking to be quite frustrating.   Sometimes it takes several matches just to get it lit.   Shortly after that it will start to gurgle and then get stopped up.

Cigar and cigarette smokers never have this problem.   Cigars and cigarettes stay lit until you're ready for them to go out.   Why can't pipe smokers enjoy the same convenience?

AUTHOR: Fair question.   There are several factors that cause the pipe to go out.   Factor one: The wall of the pipe bowl conducts heat away from the burning tobacco.   Therefore, if you stop puffing for a few moments, the pipe cools down and the fire goes out.   Solution to this problem: keep puffing gently and regularly.   Also, a pipe made from old, high quality, cured, light weight briar smokes better than one made from green, heavy, sap-filled briar, because it insulates better.

Factor two: When anything burns, water vapor is formed. In a pipe, this vapor condenses at the bottom of the bowl and tends to make the tobacco soggy.   It's worse on hot humid days. Solution: use a dry pipe.   And don't smoke on hot muggy days.

Factor three: In the summertime, the tobacco in a pouch or loosely sealed container absorbs moisture from the air, making it hard to light or keep lit. Solution: keep your tobacco in a tightly sealed container.

During the winter months, the tobacco in your pouch tends to dry out. And, sometimes, when you light it, too much of the tobacco catches on fire all at once--and you have a raging, tongue burning fire in the bowl of your pipe. Solution: if the tobacco in your pouch becomes too dry, moisten a couple of your fingers with cold water and flick the water into the pouch.

Factor four: The pipe must be properly broken in--caked from the bottom up. I think I've figured out the best way to do this. First, you place a small pinch of tobacco in the bottom of the bowl of your new pipe and smooth it down flat with your little finger. Now, the crucial part--wad up a tiny ball of tobacco, about a quarter inch in diameter, and center it in the bottom of the bowl. Continue filling the pipe a pinch at a time-- but fill it only half full. Then, after gently tamping the tobacco down, light up your pipe and smoke it all the way to the bottom-- relighting, if necessary. The little ball will force the tobacco to burn near the sides of the bowl, caking it from the bottom up. Repeat this procedure the first three or four times that you smoke your new pipe.

Incidentally, I continue to use the little ball of tobacco even after the pipe is broken in. It seems to keep the pipe drier. I think what happens is that it absorbs heat and the heat keeps water vapor from condensing in the bowl.

READER K: It's probably equivalent to a backlog in a fireplace.

AUTHOR: That's a good analogy.

READER F: How about the proper way of filling the pipe and lighting it once it's broken in?

AUTHOR: Factors five and six: According to the experts when filling your pipe you want to strive for even porosity--no lumps and no loose spots or air pockets--so that when you draw on the pipe the air travels smoothly and evenly through the tobacco. The best way to do this is, as I said, putting the tobacco in a pinch at a time and smoothing it down--and repeating the process until the pipe is full, making sure that it's packed not too tight and not too loose.

As to the proper way to light the pipe, I think most experts agree that the best thing to light your pipe with is a wooden match. At first you draw four or five deep puffs, moving the flame back and forth across the exposed tobacco to make sure the tobacco is well lit all the way across. Also, the initial deep puffs heats up the whole mass of tobacco and causes it to contract and pull away from the sides of the bowl. This makes for a milder, tastier smoke. After the initial deep puffs, continue moving the flame around and puffing gently until the match goes out or until the flame gets too close to your fingers.

When you're lighting the pipe, be careful that you don't blow back through the stem as this will blow out the match. Instead, blow out of the corners of your mouth.

After the pipe is well lit, keep puffing gently and regularly.

READER F: Why does the tobacco have to be moist? Wouldn't it burn better if it was dry?

AUTHOR: As I said earlier, if the tobacco is too dry, too much of it may catch on fire and the smoke will burn your tongue. With the proper amount of moisture and if the tobacco is packed just right--not too loose and not too tight--it will burn just across the top thin layer, while the next layer is being dried out sufficiently and heated up to the ignition point which, for tobacco, is about 750_F.

If the tobacco is too moist it mats up and loses porosity--it won't draw freely and you can't keep it lit.

READER F: One more question. How is it possible that you can smoke a pipe for thirty or forty minutes, or sometimes for an hour, while a cigar only lasts for ten to twenty minutes, even though there's two or three times as much tobacco in a cigar as there is in the bowl of a pipe?

AUTHOR: That's an interesting question--I've wondered about that myself. I think the way the tobacco is processed and cut might have something to do with it. But I don't think that's the only reason.

READER K: Let me see--I think I can explain it. It's like a banked fire. When I was a kid, one of my chores, in the wintertime, was to take care of the fire in the fireplace. The last thing I did at night was to cover the remaining hot coals and pieces of burning wood with ashes.

The next morning, when I uncovered the coals, they were still red hot. Then all I had to do to start the fire was add more kindling and a log or two and blow on it.

So, after you get your pipe well lit, the ashes and the caked walls of the pipe bowl keep the fire banked. The only time oxidation takes place is when you draw air through it.

On the other hand, a cigar gets oxygen whether you draw on it or not.

Of course, in a pipe, since the mass of tobacco is so small and the insulation is so thin, if you wait too long between puffs you won't be able to rekindle the fire without using a match.

AUTHOR: I think you may have come up with the answer.

READER L: I have a question. If smoking a pipe is so complicated and so plagued with problems and is so often a frustrating experience, why in the world would anyone want to go through the agony and the mess of trying to smoke one of the things.

As far as I'm concerned, the only really satisfying smoke-- pure pleasure and no hassle--is a good hand made cigar. The fellow that said: "A woman is only a woman, but a good cigar is a smoke," had a point.

READER D: One might say a pipe is like a wife, at times cantankerous, aggravating and mean--but if understood and treated right, can become a treasured, life-long companion and a source of joy, comfort and happiness.

A cigar is more like a one night stand--wham, bam, and thank you ma'am.

READER C: If you ask me, anyone who sucks on a pipe, a cigar, or a cigarette is just trying to return to his infancy.

READER D: Ouch!

READER B: To some American Indians, at one time, pipe smoking was a mystical or spiritual thing. The grains of tobacco represented the souls of all the things on Earth, living things (birds, fish, animals, trees, flowers, etc.) and other things as well, such as rocks, streams, mountains, etc.

The burning of the tobacco released the spirit of each being. All the spirits, represented by the smoke, would then mingle with each other and rise up to join with the Great Spirit in the sky.

AUTHOR: Yes. I read about that in the book I mentioned earlier. I think I must be partly native American. I don't do the ritual of turning to the west, holding my pipe out in front of me and putting a pinch of the holy mixture into the bowl--then repeating the process to the north, to the east and to the south.

But I do like to look around, while I'm smoking, at the trees, the clouds, the horizon and the birds and squirrels, and at people and dogs passing by. And as the smoke rises and disperses into the air, I sit back and, as the expression goes, try to become one with the universe.

Of course, sometimes while smoking my pipe, I'm thinking about this book and the chapter I'm working on or the chapters ahead. And speculating on what you the readers might have to say on the various subjects.

READER F: You still haven't told us, step by step, how to smoke a pipe all the way down using only one or two matches.

AUTHOR: There is considerable difference between the two match technique and the one match technique. With the two match method you have time to enjoy yourself. Whereas in the one match technique you have to concentrate practically the whole time on keeping the pipe lit.

First the two match method: Fill the pipe and light it, in the manner described earlier, and puff away gently and regularly. After a minute or so, tamp the ashes down lightly--drawing a bit more strongly as you do so.

By this time the fire in the bowl should be well established. And with regular puffing should keep burning for fifteen or twenty minutes.

By the time the tobacco burns down to about the halfway point, it's beginning to get too moist and it starts burning down the middle. Then it goes out, leaving pieces of tobacco clinging to the sides of the bowl.

Now, you carefully spill out some of the loose ashes, then take your pipe tool--or an ordinary sharp pointed pencil will do-- and gently loosen the pieces of tobacco from the sides of the bowl and move them into the center. Tamp down very lightly and relight. Resume regular puffing and enjoy another fifteen or twenty minutes of smoking pleasure.

Now, if you want to go for the big achievement--smoking the pipe all the way down using only one match--you really have to concentrate. And don't expect to accomplish this feat the very first time you try it.

First, make sure the weather is suitable and that your pipe is well caked and dry, and that your tobacco has the proper moisture content.

Then you proceed as described above, except that you don't wait until the pipe goes out before you start poking and moving the unburned pieces of tobacco from the sides of the bowl to the middle. In fact, you should begin about ten minutes after lighting the pipe and repeat every five or ten minutes thereafter. Remember to draw a little stronger on the pipe while performing this operation--else the poking and tamping might put out the fire.

After the tobacco burns down about halfway, spill out some of the loose ashes, as they might sift down through the tobacco and clog up the hole at the bottom of the bowl that leads to the pipe stem. Be careful not to dump the burning tobacco along with the ashes.

If after dozens of attempts, using your best briar pipe, you are still unable to smoke down to the dottle using only one match, switch to a pipe made from cherry wood. Cherry wood absorbs moisture--so your tobacco stays drier. Briar is an oily wood and does not absorb water.

Using a cherry pipe and following the prescribed procedure, you should be able to achieve the one match feat in short order. Then, with this under your belt, you can go back to your briar with a bit more confidence.

READER H (musician): Why don't you just stick to the cherry pipe and avoid altogether the hassle of a soggy pipe that won't stay lit?

READER C: The answer to that question is that pipe smokers are masochistic by nature--driven to self-torture.

AUTHOR: No, no. It's because good briar adds a rich, luxurious taste to the smoke. Whereas, a cherry wood pipe, even though it might smoke easier, has an insipid flavor compared to briar. And sometimes the cherry pipe smokes too dry and gets too hot, and tastes like burnt wood.

Anyway, getting back to what I said earlier, it's okay, once in a while, to try the one match thing--just to prove that you can still do it. But it is much more pleasurable if you don't worry about whether you use one, two, or even three matches. Enjoy the taste, watch the smoke curl upward and disappear into the air. Admire the rich color and grain of the briar. Enjoy a cup of coffee and a chat with friends, along with your smoke.

After you learn the technique of filling the pipe, lighting it, and periodically poking and tamping the tobacco--with practice you might, in time, learn to do these things automatically.

One day, you might be sitting back enjoying your pipe, surveying your surroundings, or just day dreaming, and then a little later discover that without much conscious effort, you've managed to smoke an entire pipe full of tobacco using only one single solitary match. Or maybe two--it doesn't matter.

Congratulate yourself. You have now learned the art of pipe smoking.

Chapter 9

READER F (artist--speaking to the author): In the previous chapter you intimated, several times, that pipe smoking is an art. I've always linked art with creativity. What is it that we create when we smoke a pipe?

AUTHOR: Well, if you do it right you're creating a certain amount of sensual pleasure for your taste buds and for the olfactory nerve. Also, visual pleasure from the curling smoke. But the most important thing created, perhaps, is the pacification of the spirit.

READER D (couch potato): Speaking of art, down through the years various critics, pundits, and commentators have attempted to define art and distinguish between good art and bad art. What say we have a go at it?

READER F: That's just fine with me, because I think I might have some significant and useful ideas on the subject. Especially in the categories of drawing and painting.

AUTHOR: According to my Webster's, art has to do with human creativity--making things and executing plans. We might also add the terms processing and performing.

READER E (young religious woman): I once read a quotation that said: "Art is a collaboration between the artist and God, and the less the artist does the better the art."

READER B (professor): It was said by the French novelist and critic, Andre Gide.

AUTHOR: That quotation may be of help when we get to the discussion of what is good art and what is not so good art. But first let's discuss the broad spectrum of things that might come under the heading of art.

READER B: Well, there are the so called fine arts - music, literature, drama, drawing and painting, sculpture, dance, and architecture. And then there's culinary arts, sewing arts, liberal arts, primitive arts, the art of politics.

READER A (insurance man): How about the martial arts, the art of selling. And the art of love.

AUTHOR: There's also the art of diplomacy, the art of wine making. And I suppose you could say there's an art to cutting hair, or trimming hedges, or even digging a ditch.

READER D: I guess we all agree that art involves creativity. And that the thing created can be in static form, such as a painting, a statue, a piece of architecture, or a ditch. Or it can be in sequential or episodic form such as a novel, a drama, a poem, a speech, or a piece of music.

READER B: In a so-called performing art, such as drama, who is doing the creating, the playwright or the performer? Of course the answer is both. The writer creates the script and the performer creates his interpretation of the character he plays, from his own experience, his emotions and imagination, and with the skillful use of his voice and body movement, timing and dynamics.

READER D: Also, the play director, the set director, wardrobe person, make-up artist, producer--in fact, anyone involved in the process, including the people attending the play.

AUTHOR: You used the phrase: Involved in the process. We've already agreed, I think, that any artistic endeavor has something to do with creativity. Do we also agree that it involves a process?

If so, what is the first step in the process--something that is applicable to all artistic categories? What additional steps are there? What is the anatomy common to all?

READER B: I suppose you begin with an idea. Then you develop the idea--as to content, basic form, size, scope, and duration.

READER D: When do you engage your particular muse or, in Andre Gide's case, when and how does the collaboration between God and the artist begin?

READER F: The collaboration starts early in life, before the artist becomes an artist. For a painter it's when he begins to notice the miraculous way the Great Master Painter shapes and colors the landscape and fills it with an infinite variety of detail, texture, configuration, mood, and beauty in the form of hills, valleys, the sky, trees, flowers, birds, animals, and so forth.

READER A: A great deal of the art, music, and literature being produced, today, seems to have been created in collaboration with the devil.

AUTHOR: Well, let's see what we have so far. Art begins with an idea and involves a process of creating something.

READER L (businessman): In other words--art is the process of turning idea into product.

AUTHOR: Succinctly put. And if we count an artistic performance as product, then as far as I can see, it applies to any kind of art.

READER F: Shouldn't we include materials and tools in there some place? In painting you need canvas and paint. And you need tools such as brushes, an easel, and a palette.

READER H (musician): To a music composer, a piece of paper and ink are the materials. And a piano and an ink pen are his tools. His product is a musical score. But what is the score to a symphony orchestra? Is it idea--or is it material?

READER D: I'd say it's a piece of material.

READER H: Then what represents idea?

READER D: Well, that's when the director and the symphony board get together and come up with an idea for a concert. Let's say they decide on a double dip of Beethoven. And the idea is to wake up the concert goers and stir up a bit of primal passion with Ludwig's Fifth Symphony. Then, after intermission, expand their souls and lift their spirits with the Third or the Ninth.

The score is the material. The musical instruments are the player's tools, while the whole orchestra is the tool of the conductor.

READER H: You might have a point there. But I still think the score is part of the idea. The conductor and the musicians add their own ideas on how to interpret the score, as to phrasing, tonal shading, and dynamics.

READER C (aerobics instructor): It's probably both. Let's say that to a musician the score is a piece of material containing the ideas of the composer. However, if I get the idea to bake a cake--culinary art--the materials I need are flour, sugar, salt, baking powder, eggs and flavoring. I also need a recipe. Now I don't tear out the recipe page from the cookbook and put it in the mixing bowl. Therefore, to the cook, the recipe is part of the idea, whether it's from the cookbook or from memory.

READER E (young religious woman): Reader D spoke of arousing the emotions of the concert goers and of elevating their spirits. Just how does spirituality and the emotions enter into the artistic process?

READER H: I suppose that the artist projects his own emotions and spirit into his creations and hopes to evoke similar feelings in his audiences.

READER F: The spirit is involved all the way through the process. Once I get an idea of what I want to paint--a person, an animal, still life, landscape or whatever the motif might happen to be--it takes courage to face that bare canvas. Also, desire, faith in your abilities, and a lot of will power.

READER B: When someone asked Mrs. Andrew Wyeth what her husband's Helga series was all about, she answered with one word: Love. I suppose she meant love in the pure sense. So perhaps art is the product of a love affair between the artist and whatever else is involved in his artistic endeavor--his source of inspiration, his materials, tools, instruments, and his audience.

READER E: According to the Bible, God is the Great Creator and God is Love. And without his infinite creativity and boundless love we would have no artists, no inspiration, no models or motifs, no materials and no instruments. No art.

AUTHOR: Someone once asked Louis Armstrong to define Jazz. His answer was that if you have to ask you'll never know. That might apply to any form of art. Be that as it may, I think you've come up with some illuminating comments. And despite Satchmo's admonition, I'd like to hear some discussion on the difference between good art and bad art.

READER B: It's very likely that the argument about what is good art and what is not, like many such arguments, will never become settled. But we might as well have fun trying.

To me, a good piece of art is one that is so well put together that all things in it work together to communicate the vision of the artist and the effect he wants to achieve. There are no unnecessary parts.

In order to achieve this, an artist has to be knowledgeable of the medium he's working in and of the materials, tools, and instruments that go with it. And he must have sufficient technique and skill to accomplish his artistic goals. But most of all the artist must have an active imagination. And a vision that is uniquely his, but is also one that resonates with his audiences.

READER A: What about talent?

READER F: I'm glad you brought that up. Occasionally, someone viewing my work will say to me: "I wish I could do that--you must have a God given talent."

Well, I think just about everyone is capable of doing something well, or several things, for that matter. But as I said before, you have to have the desire, the faith, and the will to apply yourself.

On a particular project, if you whet your desire, strengthen your faith--maybe pray a little--and exert your will, and keep working toward your goal, making needed changes, correcting mistakes, adding something here, taking something out there, after awhile, things seem to start falling into place. And your idea becomes reality.

For success in any artistic field (or any other field, for that matter) what you need most in the way of talent is a talent for persistence.

READER D: Getting back to the subject of good art versus bad art, could we say that good art is art concerned with and produced in the spirit of love and in collaboration with God? And bad art is that which is produced in the spirit of hate or indifference and in collaboration with the devil?

READER B: Okay. But sometimes there's a paradox. Take for example Picasso's great painting depicting the wanton destruction of the city of Guernica and of its helpless citizens, during the Spanish Civil War. I presume that it was inspired by his hatred of war and of the perpetrators of this particular bit of evil.

READER C: Depicting the horror, the tragedy, the suffering and sorrow of diabolical war, in that case, was an act of love.

For Picasso it was probably a catharsis. For the rest of us, I hope it will act as an inoculation, a vaccine, that will help to wipe out the scourge of war.

READER D: For once, I agree with you, unequivocally. I'm sure he was motivated by a sense of horror and dismay at what happened. And not by a gleeful desire to vicariously participate in the mayhem.

However, when it comes to some of his other paintings, I'm quite puzzled if not baffled. His depictions of women, in particular, seem to be derived from hatred or contempt for the fairer sex. It doesn't bother me that much when artists distort the shape of most things or when they impression-ize them, expression-ize them, or cube-ilize them. But when it comes to young women, they should always be depicted as we see them in Polynesian jungle movies--graceful, nubile, beautiful, and with gorgeous hair.

READER A: You probably wouldn't appreciate William de Kooning's "Woman #1" either, except as an investment. If art is supposed to hold up a mirror to nature, de Kooning and Picasso must have been using cracked mirrors.

READER B: In a novel or short story, or in a play, it's okay to include murder, rape, or mayhem if you make the perpetrators suffer for their transgressions, as in Macbeth. Or if you imply in some way that these things are not good and shouldn't be gotten away with.

Therefore, a piece of pornographic art that appeals to lust, sadistic mayhem and murder and which is presented in no redeeming social or spiritual context, is probably not very good art from an aesthetic point of view.

READER C: Amen. The creeps that create pornography have apparently never heard of aesthetics, or beauty, or redeeming social value. They crawl out from under their rocks and never rise above the level of carnality.

AUTHOR: Can we say that good art, even though it might contain elements of meanness, suffering, discord and dissonance, is art that adds something good, useful, and uplifting to our lives and helps us to connect harmoniously and meaningfully with the world around us?

READER B: Speaking of meaningfulness, once when I was teaching ballroom dancing, there was this lady who was a pretty good dancer but had never danced the Tango. And she wanted very much to learn it. So I showed her some of the steps. Then I switched on the recorded music--I think the piece was *La Comparsita*--and we started dancing. Almost immediately she began to bubble over with enthusiasm. Each step of the Tango seemed to move her to a higher state of euphoria and brought forth ecstatic oohs and ahs. When the music ended, I said to her: "You seem to enjoy the Tango quite a bit."

She answered: "I love it. When we were dancing, it seemed that with each beat of the music the story of my life was unfolding before me, page by page. I've never felt anything so meaningful in my whole life. Play it again."

I played more Tango music and we danced blissfully through several more chapters of her life before her lesson time was over.

Even though the Tango is probably the most sensual of ballroom dances and the beat of the music the most primal, what she felt seemed to me to be a sublimation of the sensual and the primal to something closer to the spiritual.

Perhaps that is one of the qualities that distinguishes good art from bad. The potential to sublimate our basic appetites, our fears, anxieties and hostilities into something higher and better.

AUTHOR: Good point. Incidentally, we've talked about the good and the bad. What about all the stuff in between?

For instance, when it comes to literature, some of the most popular categories, nowadays, are mystery stories and romance novels. Many of these are well written and a lot of readers find them very fascinating. But we don't usually think of them as great art.

READER D: Well, there's first rate art, second rate art, third rate and so forth. A really first rate book is one that makes you sustain a good feeling after you've read it. And one that you can recall with a glow, later on in your life.

Bad art is that which leaves an unpleasant after taste. And the in between, run of the mill stuff, might excite you or make you feel good temporarily--but there's little or no afterglow and no lasting significance.

READER K: Speaking of popular books, the all time best seller, no doubt, is the Holy Bible. Although its pages present many inspiring passages--depictions of miracles, examples of great compassion, charity and redemption--it is also strewn throughout with story after story of human cruelty and depravity. It runs the gamut from the carnage of war, mayhem, and murder, through acts of greed, gluttony, lust and debauchery--every cardinal and venial sin under the sun.

READER D: There's a couple of good reasons why the Bible is so popular. First, it has a great theme.

READER K: What is the theme?

READER D: Well, posing it in the form of a question, the theme asks: Can humanity rise above its sinful nature, its basic earthly desires and concerns, and become more God-like?

READER K: Okay. And what is the second reason?

READER D: The second reason is that it also happens to have a very good plot.

READER B: The Bible has a plot? Hm-m. So, what is the plot?

READER D: The plot is as follows: Humanity meets Paradise; humanity loses Paradise; humanity seeks and finds pathway back to Paradise.

READER B: I suppose, with a stretch, you could describe the Bible in those terms. But I'm afraid that a great many members of the human population haven't found that pathway-- or else they've found it and discovered that it's a bit too straight and narrow.

READER K: And more than a few of them, it seems, would rather travel in the fast lane, on the highway to hell.

I have a question. Is the Bible the textbook we must use in order to learn the most important art of all--the art of living? Were churches and synagogues set up for the purpose of teaching this discipline? If not, then, where do we go to learn the art?

READER D: You should know the answer to that question... Remember? You go to Samoa.

READER K: Yes. Of course.

Chapter 10

AUTHOR: If the art of living is the most important art of all, let's use this chapter to talk about it. We might get lucky and come up with some good basic ideas that we can pass on. Not everyone has the time or the wherewithal to go to Samoa or New Zealand.

As is our custom, let's begin by putting together a wide ranging list of the different forms of life. Then we'll try to determine what it is that all forms of life have in common.

The premise of this book is that, when you're dealing with a subject, the most important things that you need to know about the subject are the characteristics that all forms of it have in common. And that the way you handle these primal factors is most important in determining the success or failure of your endeavor.

READER B (professor): We normally think of life as being organic--animal or vegetable. And we usually say that a plant or animal is dead when it ceases to function organically.

However, we often refer to inorganic objects as having a life.

READER A (insurance man): You're right, Professor. The IRS says that when you're figuring depreciation on business vehicles, that an automobile has a four-year life. A frame building is usually figured on a twenty-five year life. Another type of life is the life of a contract. In the insurance business, there's whole life and term life.

READER D (couch potato): As the Professor said, we normally think that life ends when a thing ceases to function organically. But not always. For example, we might say that Mozart lives on in his music. Or Edison in his inventions. Shakespeare in his plays and sonnets. And of course to vast numbers of his fans, Elvis Presley is still very much alive.

AUTHOR: Well, there is life and there's afterlife. According to Reader A's examples, a life has something to do with a time span.

Can we say that a particular life is the duration span of an entity? And that its life ceases when the entity disintegrates?

And that it's afterlife exists in the effect it had on its environment? And in the memories of other entities? And in the reminders it left behind?

READER B: What do you mean by the disintegration of an entity?

AUTHOR: Well, take for example a rock. A particular rock is an entity. But if you crush it into tiny pieces it becomes gravel. It is no longer recognizable as the entity it was before.

READER B: How about organic entities? For example, an eighty year old human being doesn't have much resemblance to the infant he or she once was. And we learned in grade school that we get a whole new physical body about every seven years. So what is there in an eighty year old person that has been around for that many years?

READER D: That's a hard question, Professor. It's questions like that can give a body a headache.

READER E (young religious woman): The answer to your question is the person's spirit or soul. And it lives on, even after the body has turned to dust.

READER D: Yes, of course. Now the big question: Is our soul always the same--or does it change and grow? The dictionary says that an entity is something that exists. But it doesn't say that it exists in a completely static form. We humans are apparently not static--we seem to be on a course of becoming. And we become ourselves, I think through a process of give and take between ourselves and the rest of creation.

READER M: NOT LONG AGO I CAME UPON THE THOUGHT THAT MY LIFE IS AN AFFAIR BETWEEN XO AND ME--AN AFFAIR EVERY MOMENT CONTINUOUS AND INFINITE.

READER E: We are born weak and helpless in body. And we're born raw and narrow in spirit. The body grows larger and stronger by receiving proper nurturing and through proper exercise, and by avoiding things that are harmful to the body.

Our spirit grows and becomes better through harmonious interaction with other souls, and by exercising it with acts of love and by overcoming evil with goodness, and by infusions of the Holy Spirit, through prayer and worship.

READER D: Now, for the really big question: What happens to the spirit when the body dies? Will I still be me, after I die?

READER B: According to the Old Testament, the spirit of life comes from God, and the spirit never dies. Perhaps, after the body dies, our spirit, again, becomes one with the Holy Spirit--our consciousness one with God's. And we'll know the answer to all questions. And our existence on Earth will be just a memory in the mind of God.

READER D: Or we might live on as angels in Heaven, keeping our own separate spiritual identities and consciousness, and rejoin with our loved ones who have gone on before.

READER A: What about the bad guys--the mean spirited, self-centered, self-serving sinners who never took out any celestial insurance?

READER D: The unredeemed go to that other place--and grow horns and a tail. And about the only thing they'll learn, when they get there, is that it's mighty hot down there. Incidentally, what is this celestial insurance you mentioned?

READER A: You might call it the eternal life policy. You pay for the premiums by confessing your sins and seeking forgiveness for them--and by changing your way of living.

READER C: A lot of people, nowadays, are claiming they have evidence that we have more than one life. Dozens in fact. And that, after the body dies, the soul floats around for a while in a peaceful, highly spiritual place, then is reborn in a new earthly body.

This reincarnation takes place over and over, until the soul is perfected to the level necessary to achieve nirvana or spiritual bliss, they say.

READER B: There must not be any convincing proof of their claims, else we'd be hearing more about it.

Our concerns about the concepts of good and evil and of life after death are of primal interest to most people. And, in general, we think that humans are the only beings that can choose between good and evil--or make any kind of choices. And that other forms of life react by instinct--for the most part like pre-programmed robots.

There are many people, however--storytellers, artists, cartoonists, religious sects, and New Age thinkers--who express the notion that all forms of life have souls and can think and feel and reason--everything from humans to dogs and cats, cockroaches, fish, spiders, plants, rocks, cars, door knobs, coat hangers--you name it.

READER E: In Luke, chapter nineteen, it relates that when someone asked Jesus to quiet his multitude of followers, who were rejoicing and shouting praises to God, Jesus said: "I tell you that, if these should hold their peace, the stones would immediately cry out."

READER F (artist): If you were to take up drawing and painting, you might be inclined to believe that things have souls. To paint a picture of something you have to concentrate on your subject to the point that you establish a kind of rapport with it-- even if the subject is just an inanimate object.

You become intimate with its shape, its color and texture, the play of light and shadow, the nature of its being, and the purpose and significance of its existence in the scheme of things. And you try to put your perceptions down on paper or canvas.

Artists usually like to paint old things, things that have been used or that have been affected, over time, by their environment. Such things seem to have more life in them--more soul.

AUTHOR: The implication of what you just said is that the soul of an entity has something to do with the way it's used. For example, a bowl is used for holding or containing something. That's its purpose. An automobile is used to transport people and things. A knife is used to cut or carve something. But what is the purpose of humans?

READER D: Well, Reader F has the soul of an artist. His purpose in life is to paint pictures. Reader A's purpose is to insure us against financial catastrophe, in exchange for a small monthly premium. And Reader C's purpose is to cause physical pain to her aerobics customers.

READER C (aerobics instructor): I suppose your purpose in life is to sit on a couch.

READER D: And a couch's purpose is to be sat upon. It's a symbiotic relationship that we have.

READER E (young religious woman): The purpose for each one of us, as humans, is to find out what God wants us to do, then do it to the best of our ability.

READER B: Reader F alluded to an awareness of the significance of the existence or life of an entity. It was mentioned, earlier, that life is an affair between an entity and the rest of creation--or something to that effect. What is the basic significance of a life, any life, in the general scheme of things?

READER M: THE PRIME SIGNIFICANCE OF THIS AFFAIR IS THAT IT OCCASIONS XO AND ME TO BECOME OURSELVES AND EACH OTHER TO SOME EXTENT.

AUTHOR: You again, with another bold, declarative statement. But what does it mean? Who are you? And who is XO? And why are you using all capital letters?

READER M: Please let me explain. I was following your dialogue--with considerable interest, I might add--and I began to notice that several of the ideas expressed reminded me of something I wrote, some years back, when I was studying philosophy. It's called "BETWEEN XO AND ME," and consists of thirty or more statements. I wanted the style to be boldly declarative, and I figured using all capitals would help achieve that result.

AUTHOR: And who--or what--is XO? And how is it pronounced, exactly? Is it pronounced as if it were spelled Zoe?

READER M: Yes. Or, as if it were spelled XEAUX. As to who or what XO is, you'll have to figure that out for yourself.

READER D: And why is that?

READER M: Well, in my study of philosophy, it seemed that each new philosopher that came along would, first, endeavor to disprove all other philosophers. And, following that, would lay out his own version of the Truth.

Sooner or later, however, his ideas would be trampled on and mangled by succeeding seekers of the truth. What a pity, I thought. All these fellows probably have the truth inside them but when they try to state it, in so many words, it is never totally convincing--it never goes unchallenged.

In fact, quite often, writers of pure fiction seem to be more accepted as purveyors of the truth than philosophers.

Anyway, wanting to become a philosopher but not wanting my ideas to suffer the usual fate, I decided that instead of trying to overwhelm the world with clear, precise, and logical articulation of my notions of the truth, I would attempt to evoke the truth that lies within everyone by purposefully presenting my ideas in a fuzzy, imprecise and, sometimes, ambivalent manner.

My hope was that anyone contemplating my work would try to flesh it out with their own truth. And that my work would be appreciated--not denigrated.

READER B: Has anyone read it? If so, has there been any interesting truths brought to light?

READER M: I'm not sure about how much truth has been evoked. But, over the years, I've gotten some fascinating responses from people who have read it. I've been accused of being blasphemous, sacrilegious, sophomoric, a heathen, and an existentialist, among other things. XO has been defined as a woman, my environment, God, Satan, the universal spirit, my alter ego, and the all pervading nothingness.

And there were some who, by their facial expressions, seem to be wondering whether the work was supposed to be serious or merely tongue in cheek--or whether or not my mentes was fully compus. Others who read it didn't seem to be impressed with it, one way or the other.

READER D: What is your own opinion of it?

READER M: My opinion? Well, I won't comment on the profundity of the ideas or the originality. Just the style. My aim was to distill each idea down to its purest form, with a minimum of imagery, and to couch it in a cadence that would match and enhance, dynamically, the character of the idea. The result might not be 100 proof but it has a pretty good kick to it, I think.

READER A: So, can we hear the rest of it? Or do we have to buy the book?

READER M: There's no book. It's not long enough for a book--only about 1,200 words. I made a few copies of it, but, offhand, I don't remember where I put them. However, I've got it memorized and I could recite it for you, if you like.

AUTHOR: Please do. If the two items you've already recited are an indication, we may be in for a treat. And if the rest of them aren't published in some way, the world of wisdom might be missing out on a string of philosophical pearls.

In fact, if it's okay with you, we'll let it become the next chapter in this book.

READER M: It's fine with me. And thank you--you are very gracious.

AUTHOR: Before we sign off on this chapter, there's something that I'd like to discuss further. Since our belief and attitude about what happens to us when our body dies can affect how we conduct our lives, here on Earth, it might be useful to describe and list some of the ideas that have been generated, over the last few thousand years, about the subject.

One idea--not necessarily the most prevalent--is that when the body expires so does the conscious spirit. Life is over, finis, kaput. And that we experience Heaven or Hell only during our life here on Earth.

READER M: One view of how to spend that lifetime is the Hedonistic view--pursuing pleasure and happiness. Another view--pursuing virtue, reason, and inner peace, and remaining indifferent to pleasure and pain. Personally, sometimes I feel the need to be reasonably Hedonistic and, other times, to practice a modicum of stoicism.

READER D: In the western world, I think the most widely held view is that you only live one earthly life and if you have been good or if you have been redeemed, you go to live, eternally, in Heaven. If you've been bad and are unredeemed, you spend eternity in Hell.

READER C: However, more and more people are subscribing to the Hindu belief that the soul doesn't die with the body nor is it limited to only one earthly life. Some psychologists and psychiatrists believe there are strong indications, if not virtual proof, that this is true. And that neuroses, obsessive behavior, and certain physical illnesses in some of their patients had root causes in previous lives. And that the patients have been cured through regression therapy that involved going back and reliving portions of a previous life.

READER B: Still, there is no actual proof that reincarnation is a reality. Here's the usual procedure: The doctor hypnotizes his patient and asks him or her to go back to the original cause of the problem that the patient is being treated for. Sometimes a patient describes an incident that supposedly happened hundreds or thousands of years before, in a land far away, when he or she was in another body. The descriptions for that time and place are deemed to be accurate, but, there was no way the patient, it is claimed, could have learned the information by personal observation or by reading or hearing about it, during their present lifetime.

An alternate explanation for what happens is that, somewhere in our brain, there is an encyclopedic memory storage bin of everything that ever happened anywhere, anytime, in the universe. Or that the brain can access such a memory bank. And that when the therapist asks the patient to go back to the origin of his or her problem, the patient flips through the file, until a likely incident is found and offers it to the therapist, sometimes embellished by the creative portion of the patient's brain.

Whether it is this theory or the reincarnation theory, or a combination of the two, as a therapeutic process, it seems to work.

READER D: The reason it works might be because the therapist and his patient both believe that they have really discovered the original cause of the patient's problem--and that it happened in a previous life. And, since it happened so long ago, it's time to sluff it off and quit suffering from it.

READER G (reporter): Not only are people going back into the past, allegedly, but there are purportedly documented instances of people seeing into the future. If so, that lends credence to the idea of predestination--that our lives are pre-ordained. If it's true that our lives are pre-ordained, then the "moving finger," referred to by Omar Khayyam, doesn't write-- the story of our life is already written. The moving finger only guides our eyes across the pages.

READER L: Well, which is it: Just one life of a few years here on earth, and that's it?

Or, one earthly life plus eternal life in heaven or hell? Or, many lives, through reincarnation, until we get it right and achieve nirvana?

Or, is it that our destiny is out of our hands--every second of it already worked out?

READER B: As yet, there's no cognitive or observable way of knowing, for certain.

READER E: There is a way of knowing. But it doesn't involve the five earthly senses. You have to use a higher faculty: It's called faith.

READER D: Well, let's see now. We've defined life. And discussed the significance of it. And we have speculated on life after death. But, as yet, we haven't said much about the art of living. Reader E may have come up with step number one: Find out what the Good Lord wants you to do. Then, get on with it.

What I would like to know is--how does one find out what one is supposed to do in life? And how do you straighten out a messed up life? Plato wrote that "a life unexamined is not worth living." But he didn't tell us how to conduct such an examination.

READER L: In the business world we sometimes do what we refer to as a comprehensive review of the whole company business. Or we might conduct an agonizing reappraisal of a particular operation or project.

Perhaps we can come up with some such approach on a personal basis. Call it the agonizing, comprehensive, self-review method.

AUTHOR: Sounds like a splendid idea. But let's do it in chapter twelve. I'm anxious to hear more about the affair between XO and Reader M.

READER M: Before I present it to you, I would like to request that there be no discussion afterward. And no questions, to me, about it. Each reader should search within himself as to the meaning of the various statements.

AUTHOR: Fair enough. No problem. If that is your wish, so be it. Now, if you're ready, let's hear: BETWEEN XO AND ME, by Reader M.

Chapter 11

READER M: Thank you. As you will see, the statements are numbered in Roman numerals from I to XXXIX:

I

NOT LONG AGO, I CAME UPON THE THOUGHT THAT MY LIFE IS AN AFFAIR BETWEEN XO AND ME--- AN AFFAIR, EVERY MOMENT CONTINUOUS AND INFINITE.

II

SOMETIMES THIS AFFAIR SEEMS TO GO ALONG UNDER MY CONTROL--AND SOMETIMES UNDER XO'S CONTROL IN SOME SITUATIONS NEITHER XO NOR I EXERCISE VERY MUCH APPARENT CONTROL--AND MY LIFE IS A SEEMING CHAOS.

IV

OTHER TIMES WE STRUGGLE FOR CONTROL-- AND MY LIFE IS A CONFLICT.

V

ANYTHING I WANT FROM XO I CAN GET, WITH OCCASIONAL EXCEPTIONS, BY APPLYING MYSELF IN ONE WAY OR ANOTHER

VI

AND I CAN DO ALMOST ANYTHING I WISH TO XO. BUT I MUST BEAR THE ENSUING CONSEQUENCES. AND OF COURSE THERE ARE SOME THINGS, IT SEEMS, XO STOPS ME FROM DOING ALTOGETHER.

VII

BUT WHAT XO STOPS ME FROM DOING TODAY, XO MAY LET ME DO TOMORROW. AND WHAT XO HOLDS FROM ME NOW XO MAY SURRENDER IN A LITTLE WHILE.

VIII

AND THAT WHICH APPLIES IN ONE QUARTER OF THIS AFFAIR APPLIES MORE OR LESS IN ANY QUARTER.

IX

IN MY EVERYDAY THINKING, XO IS PARTLY REAL AND PARTLY PHANTASY. XO IS PARTLY OF THE PAST, PARTLY OF THE PRESENT, AND PARTLY OF THE FUTURE.

XO IS VERY NEAR AND XO IS FAR AWAY. AND XO INCLUDES THE VOID AS WELL AS THE EXTANT.

X

BUT WHETHER A PARTICULAR BIT OF XO IS REAL OR PHANTASY, NEAR OR FAR, LARGE OR SMALL, OR WHETHER IT IS PAST, PRESENT, OR FUTURE, IS

EXTANT OR VOID: IT CAN STILL AFFECT ME--
SERIOUSLY OR OTHERWISE.

XI

I FIND IT EXTREMELY DIFFICULT, IF NOT
IMPOSSIBLE, TO TELL PRECISELY WHERE XO LEAVES
OFF AND I BEGIN OR WHICH PART IS XO AND WHICH
PART IS ME.

XII

THE PRIME SIGNIFICANCE OF THIS AFFAIR IS THAT
IT OCCASIONS XO AND ME TO BECOME OURSELVES
AND EACH OTHER TO SOME EXTENT.

XIII

ANOTHER SIGNIFICANCE OF THIS AFFAIR IS THAT
IT OCCASIONS XO AND ME TO DISCOVER OURSELVES
AND EACH OTHER, TO SOME EXTENT.

XIV

ANOTHER SIGNIFICANCE OF THIS AFFAIR IS THAT
IT OCCASIONS XO AND ME TO DESTROY OURSELVES
AND EACH OTHER TO SOME EXTENT.

XV

ANOTHER SIGNIFICANCE OF THIS AFFAIR IS THAT
IT OCCASION XO AND ME TO PERPETUATE
OURSELVES AND EACH OTHER TO SOME EXTENT.

XVI

XO AND I BECOME OURSELVES, XO AND I DISCOVER OURSELVES, XO AND I DESTROY OURSELVES, XO AND I PERPETUATE OURSELVES THROUGH A PROCESS OF GIVE AND TAKE—OF INTERCOURSE--BETWEEN XO AND ME.

XVII

I CANNOT DEFINE XO IN THE ABSOLUTE. I CAN NEVER GET FAR ENOUGH AWAY TO VIEW XO AS A WHOLE. FOR, WHEREVER I GO, I'M STILL ENCOMPASSED BY XO. IT'S LIKE BEING PERPETUALLY TO NEAR THE TREES TO SEE THE FOREST.

XVIII

AND IF I LOOK TOO CLOSELY AT XO--AS THROUGH A GREAT MAGNIFIER--XO BECOMES TRANSPARENT AND SEEMS TO DISAPPEAR.

XIX

AND IF I SEEK THE ABSOLUTE ANSWER THROUGH ARMCHAIR LOGIC, OR FROM WEIGHTY TOMES, OR FROM LEARNED PROFESSORS, OR FROM SPOUTING DOGMATISTS I BECOME VERY TIRED. IT'S LIKE TRYING TO WALK THROUGH HIP DEEP MUD.

XX

I CAN GET A TRUE GLIMPSE OF XO, HOWEVER, BY LOOKING AT WHATEVER IS BEFORE ME--BUT WITH

EYES FOCUSED A LITTLE BEYOND OR A LITTLE IN FRONT OF THAT WHICH IS BEFORE ME.

XXI

AND I CAN HEAR THE VOICE OF XO BY LISTENING FROM A SECLUDED PLACE. IT IS A RINGING, HUMMING, SOUGHING SOUND.

XXII

AND I CAN FEEL THE SPIRIT OF XO BY BECOMING ATTUNED. AND I BECOME ATTUNED BY BEING STILL. FOR, WHEN I STOP WHAT I'M DOING, STOP WHAT I'M THINKING, AND STOP WHAT I'M FEELING, WHEN I AM STILL, THE SPIRIT COMES STEALING THROUGH ME-- ANYWHERE, ANYTIME-- LIKE THE EFFECT OF A GOOD WINE.

XXIII

AND I CAN DISCERN MEANINGFULNESS IN THIS AFFAIR WHEN TOGETHER, XO AND I, FREELY AND WITHOUT RESERVATION, PURSUE IT TO THE FULLEST.

XXIV

FOR PRACTICAL PURPOSES I CONSIDER XO AS BEING ONE PART IDEA, ONE PART SPIRIT, AND ONE PART ENERGY/MATTER.

XXV

SOMETIMES THIS AFFAIR BRINGS ME CLOSE TO DANGER: LEADS ME ON AS IT WERE TO DANGER WROUGHT PRECIPICES AND INTO HAUNTING VALLEYS SET WITH TRAPS.

XXVI

WHATEVER I DO, WHETHER IT IS A LITTLE THING OR A BIG THING, AFFECTS XO FOREVER. AND WHATEVER XO DOES AFFECTS ME.

XXVII

SOMETIMES IT HAPPENS: XO GETS IN AN UNPLEASANT MOOD. STORMS AT ME AND THREATENS ME FOR NO READILY APPARENT REASON. AND ALL MY ATTEMPTS TO PLACATE XO AT SUCH TIMES ARE FUTILE.

SO I TAKE WHATEVER MEASURES ARE NECESSARY TO PROTECT MYSELF. TAKE WHAT COMFORT I CAN FIND. THEN I WAIT FOR XO'S MOOD TO CHANGE.

XXVIII

IF I SAY THERE IS MORE BAD THAN GOOD IN THIS AFFAIR AND THAT IT WILL BRING ME ONLY MISERY, WHO CAN PROVE ME WRONG?

XXIX

IF, ON THE OTHER HAND, I SAY XO IS MORE GOOD THAN BAD AND THAT THIS AFFAIR CAN BE DEEPLY SATISFYING, WHO CAN PROVE ME WRONG THERE?

XXX

PERIODICALLY I AM REMINDED OF THIS FACT: XO SPELLED BACKWARDS IS OX.

XXXI

THERE ARE TIMES IN THE COURSE OF THIS AFFAIR WHEN I FIND MYSELF IN A QUAGMIRE OF DESPAIR AND FRUSTRATION FROM WHICH I CANNOT ESCAPE BY ANY CONSCIOUS ACTION OR BY ANY CONSCIOUS LINE OF THOUGHT.

MY ONLY RECOURSE IS TO SLEEP, TO BECOME UNCONSCIOUS FOR AWHILE.

XXXII

SOMETIMES I MAKE A DELIBERATE ATTEMPT TO GET AWAY FROM XO. BUT THE HARDER I TRY TO ESCAPE, THE CLOSER XO SEEMS TO PRESS IN ON ME.

XXXIII

AND OTHER TIMES, WHEN I SEEK A MORE INTIMATE RELATIONSHIP, XO BECOMES ELUSIVE.

XXXIV

I MUST REMEMBER NOT TO PRESS TOO MUCH WHEN XO IS NOT INCLINED TOWARD ME. AND, CONVERSELY, TO BE MORE TOLERANT WHEN XO SEEKS ME OUT.

XXXV

I CAN POSSESS XO SEVERAL WAYS: XO CAN BE MINE TO HAVE AND TO HOLD: XO CAN BE MINE TO USE: XO CAN BE MINE TO WITNESS: XO CAN BE MINE TO THINK ABOUT.

XXXVI

THE ONLY TIME I SUFFER ANY UNPLEASANT ANXIETY IN THIS AFFAIR, IT SEEMS, IS WHEN I BECOME TOO MUCH CONCERNED WITH SOME PARTICULAR FACET OR FACETS AND NEGLECT THE WHOLE.

XXXVII

I CAN FEEL A CERTAIN CONTENTMENT -- AND SOMETIMES EXULTATION -- WHEN I LINK HARMONIOUSLY THE PART OF XO AT HAND, THE AFFAIR AT HAND, AND MYSELF TO THE GREATER XO AND TO THE GREATER AFFAIR.

XXXVIII

WHATEVER I LOOK FOR IN THIS AFFAIR, OR IN XO, OR IN MYSELF I CAN USUALLY FIND IF I AM

PERSISTENT. BUT WHETHER WHAT I'M LOOKING FOR IS THERE TO BEGIN WITH OR WHETHER IT IS CREATED ONLY AS I SEEK IT, I'M NEVER SURE.

XXXIX

AND I CAN'T SAY FOR SURE WHEN THIS AFFAIR BEGAN OR WHEN IT WILL END. UNLESS I SAY IT ENDS --AND BEGINS--THIS INSTANT.

Chapter 12

AUTHOR: Chapter eleven ends and chapter twelve--having to do with examining the unexamined life--commences.

READER F (artist): Before we get down to business, I'd like to ask this question: Why is it that many people appear to have no problem in getting on with their lives. As kids, they do well in school, go out for sports or play in the band. They participate in various after school activities. Later on, they choose a career, prepare for it and get on with it. They fall in love, get married, have kids, invest in a home, buy insurance. They cut the grass and wash the car and keep the house in good repair. They do all this, apparently, without making a big to-do about it.

On the other hand, there are those who engage in a lot of pondering, agonizing, and soul-searching, but seem unable to get a good life going, even with the help of expert counselors and consultants. Why is that?

READER D (couch potato): Now why did you have to ask that--just when I was thinking that we might put together a review method that could get me up off this couch and into a more active life-style?

READER C (aerobics instructor): If we can come up with a system that can do <u>that</u>, we can change the world.

READER A (insurance man): What Reader F seems to be suggesting is that self-review won't help the losers of the world and that the winner types don't need it. Maybe, maybe not. But there are a lot of people in between who are interested in improving their lives, who wonder if they are living up to their potential, or if they've set goals that are too low or too high.

READER K (retired farmer): Living a good life, some people say, is doing the best you can with what you have.

READER L (business man): If that's true, then you need a comprehensive knowledge of what you have. That means taking inventory of all your assets and liabilities--intangible as well as tangible. Everything in every nook and cranny of your life.

READER G (reporter): I think the first step should be to make a list of all the things you are interested in, committed to, responsible for, worried about, or hung up on.

READER B (professor): Great suggestion. Let's call that Phase One. Since I've had some experience in devising college study courses, maybe I can be of help in putting our ideas together in a workable form.

AUTHOR: Excellent. Could you elaborate?

READER B: Well, if it's agreeable to start with Reader G's suggestion, here is how I would lay it out through Phase One:

KNOW YOURSELF

A Comprehensive Self-Review Method

The unexamined life is not worth livin--Plato

The purpose of this review is to help you examine your own life in an in-depth and comprehensive way. Spend ample time on each step before going to the next.

PHASE I

Step 1. COMMITMENTS AND RESPONSIBILITIES: List all commitments and responsibilities, such as your marriage, children, job, religious commitment, political commitments, club memberships, causes, etc. Examine how you feel about them. Think about which ones you would like to strengthen or do better at, and which ones you'd like to reduce or eliminate.

Step 2. PROBLEMS AND CONFLICTS: Make a list of all current problems, conflicts, concerns, and hang ups, such as family problems, on the job problems, financial, health, behavior, etc. Assess the seriousness of each.

Step 3. AMBITIONS, DESIRES, AND STRONG INTERESTS: List your ambitions, passions, desires, and strong interests. Examples: To get established in a good career, to get married, have children, buy a home, paint pictures, to build something, learn to play a musical instrument, travel abroad, improve your golf score, write a book, seek public office, etc.

Step 4. OTHER INTERESTS: List anything else that you are interested in, such as sports, hobbies, community work, education courses, friendships, minor pleasures, social life, etc.

AUTHOR: Very good, Professor. I like the way this is shaping up.

READER A: Question: When compiling these lists, are we supposed to write them down?

READER B: I would think so. Or you could use your computer.

READER A: Well, there might be some things in a person's life that he or she would be a bit skittish about putting down on paper. Something that could be embarrassing, or worse, if someone were to read it.

READER D: Good point. And these are the kind of things that need examining. Perhaps, when listing such an item, you can write down a word that will readily remind you of it but will not reveal anything to anyone else. Let's say you cheated on you income tax and that you were feeling guilty about it. Just write `Tax thing' down on your list. Later on, when you examine that particular concern, you can resolve whether to pay up and relieve your conscience--or not pay and remain a tax cheat.

READER L: Or you could use the password option on your computer.

READER B: Now that little problem has been taken care of, does anyone have a suggestion for Phase Two?

READER G: Well, as Reader L suggested, we need to list our assets and liabilities. Along with that, we could list our accomplishments, awards, certificates, diplomas, and so forth. Also jobs we have held and other money-making endeavors. Our good experiences and bad experiences.

READER B: That would be appropriate. These lists would consist of objective data--facts and information-- needed to deal realistically with concerns listed in Phase One.

PHASE II

Step 1. ACCOMPLISHMENTS, AWARDS, AND HONORS: List all accomplishments, achievements, awards, diplomas, certificates, trophies and so forth, from childhood on.

Step 2. JOBS HELD: Make a list of all the paid jobs you've ever held, such as paper boy, salesman, doctor, lawyer, radio announcer, soldier, dish-washer, nurse, typist, teacher, and so forth.

Step 3. OTHER MONEY MAKING ENDEAVORS: List other endeavors that have provided you with money, such as investments, contests, gambling, art or craft work, cutting grass, washing cars, baby sitting, consulting, selling personal items, and so forth.

Step 4. UNPAID JOBS: Make a list of useful things you've done that you didn't get paid for, such as home repairs, lawn work, gardening, farm work, school projects, making signs or posters, working on cars, volunteer work, and so forth.

Step 5. TALENTS, ABILITIES, AND SKILLS: List such things as public speaking, writing, art, music, math, mechanical ability, bookkeeping, carpentry, knitting, sewing, cooking, any job related skill.

A talent is something you have a potential for, an ability is something you're pretty good at. A skill is something you are very good at.

Step 6. FINANCIAL ASSETS: List all cash assets, income resources, securities, real estate, personal property, jewelry, art objects, collections, and so forth.

Step 7. FINANCIAL LIABILITIES: Debts, mortgages, unpaid bills, inadequate income, inadequate insurance, inadequate savings.

Step 8. PERSONALITY AND CHARACTER ASSETS: List words that describe your good qualities, such as stable, honest, responsible, well mannered, affectionate, even tempered, generous, patient, and so forth.

Step 9. PERSONALITY AND CHARACTER LIABILITIES: Bad habits, annoying mannerisms, dishonesty, irresponsibility, bad temper, overly critical of others, inconsiderate, absent minded, rash, mean, selfish, impatient, poor personal hygiene.

Step 10. PHYSICAL ASSETS: Good looks, good health, physical strength, agility, keen senses, and so forth.

Step 11. PHYSICAL LIABILITIES: Poor health, unattractiveness, too short, too tall, too fat or skinny, afflictions, poor or weak physical condition.

Step 12. MISTAKES AND FAILURES: List things you've done that you think were mistakes. List things you think you've failed at. List things you regret having done. Things that you regret not having done.

Step 13. GOOD EXPERIENCES: List or recall all the good, interesting, exciting, unusual, and pleasant experiences you can remember, from earliest memories on.

Step 14. BAD EXPERIENCES: List or recall all your bad experiences, accidents, illnesses, frightening incidents, wrongs committed against you, and so forth.

AUTHOR: A splendid, comprehensive job, Professor. Anyone compiling that much information about himself would have enough information to write a book, or several books, about himself.

READER D: There are five and a half billion stories in the naked world.

READER G: It's been said that you are what you think. But a lot could be said for the notion that you are what you do and what you've done.

READER C: I agree. Especially in the eyes of others. I've found that people tend to think of you much more in terms of what you do than what you say or what you think.

READER L: In the business world, when it comes to hiring, management wants to know what kind of person you are, before giving you a job. They make this determination by looking at your resume and through references and recommendations. And through face to face interviews.

READER G: Could you elaborate on that?

READER L: Yes. Before hiring you, an employer might want to know: Are you a doer or a dawdler? A leader or a follower? Constructive thinker or a worrier?

Are you a creative thinker or a daydreamer? Producer or just a consumer? Solid citizen with roots or just a drifter and a bum?

If you ask these questions of yourself, your answers are apt to be somewhat subjective. To increase objectivity, you should refer back to the information in Phase II.

READER B: Okay. I think I've got our next phase. How's this?

PHASE III

WHAT ARE YOU?

1. DOER OR DAWDLER? Doers like to keep busy at physical or mental tasks or activities. If there is something to be done, they get to it right away, using standard methods or systems, or else planning as they go along.

Dawdlers have difficulty getting started or following through on anything.

2. PRODUCER OR CONSUMER? For our purposes, here, a producer is one who produces, in goods or services, more than he consumes. A consumer is one who consumes more than he produces.

3. LEADER OR FOLLOWER? Leaders are assertive, are able to make timely decisions, and are persuasive and able to motivate other people.

Followers may be industrious, intelligent, ambitious, but are not as assertive as leaders, and may be reluctant to assume responsibility, or make decisions.

4. CONSTRUCTIVE THINKER OR WORRIER? Constructive thinkers examine the facts, consider options, and devise practical plans and schedules. Worriers engage in fuzzy, unproductive thinking.

5. CREATIVE THINKER OR DAYDREAMER? Creative thinkers come up with new and useful ideas and viable new ways

of doing things. Daydreamer's thinking is shallow and less viable.

6. SOLID CITIZEN OR DRIFTER? The solid citizen puts down roots, takes on responsibilities, meets his obligations, is a good neighbor, pays taxes, helps his community, participates in civic and cultural activities, and so forth.

A drifter is reluctant to take on responsibilities and has little sense of belonging. He is concerned with the bare necessities and whims of the moment.

Note: In some areas of your life you may tend to be one thing, and in other areas, the opposite. For instance, you may be a doer at the office and a dawdler at doing chores around the home, and so forth.

READER D: Neat job, Professor. However, you left out a couple of things. Are you a master or a slave? A phony or the real McCoy? A stick in the mud or a wild and crazy guy?

READER C: How about this: Are you a workaholic or a couch potato?

READER D: Question. If all I do is successfully manage my inherited property and my investment folio, am I a producer or am I a consumer?

READER A: You are a producer. But your investments might be more productive if you turned them over to a professional.

READER C: Perhaps Reader D could become a productive couch potato.

READER D: Sounds interesting. But how?

READER C: Get a job as a TV critic, movie critic, or book reviewer.

READER D: Hey! Not a bad idea. I have some writing ability--I won an essay contest in high school.

AUTHOR: Well, what do you know? Our review method seems to be working even though we're still in the process of putting it together.

READER L: Another thing we should consider is the question of attitude. I heard a quote, the other day, to the effect that you can believe that you are going to succeed or you can believe that you will fail--and that you are right, either way.

READER C: Yes. If you can develop a positive, optimistic attitude about yourself and about the world around you--and if you apply yourself properly--life will usually treat you well.

A persistently negative or pessimistic attitude will make your life turn sour.

READER A: Another type is the fatalistic attitude--the belief that what will be will be. And there's also the "dog eat dog" attitude.

READER B: No doubt, each of us could benefit from a bit of attitude examination and adjustment.

PHASE IV

WHAT IS YOUR ATTITUDE TOWARD LIFE?

1. Do you believe there is more good than bad in your life and in the world in general, and that by applying yourself, and with a little help from your friends or a higher power, your life can be a satisfying and successful affair?

2. Do you believe there is more bad than good, and that your life is bound to be a failure? If so, try to determine the ratio of bad to good. Is it 60 to 40? 30 to 70? 99 to 1?

3. Do you believe that what will be will be--so why worry?

4. Do you believe it's a "dog eat dog" world, and that you'd better take all you can, by hook or crook, before you get taken?

NOTE: Sometimes, you may have a positive attitude, and at other times a negative, even desperate attitude, depending on a particular set of events or a given situation.

READER L: Another facet of the personality (or it might be the outward manifestation of attitude) is your disposition. A good way to find out what kind of disposition you have is to observe how you react when something doesn't go the way you prefer. Do you whine or cry about it? Do you just grin and bear it? Blow your top?

READER B: Good category. It's something I've thought about.

PHASE V

WHAT KIND OF DISPOSITION DO YOU HAVE?

A clue to your disposition is the way you react when something doesn't go your way. Do you blow your top? Do you immediately try to blame someone else? Are you a crybaby? Do you get sick? Sulk or withdraw? Become sarcastic? Try to make a joke? Resort to violence or intimidation?

Do you over-react? Under react? Or do you react more or less in a reasonable manner, according to the nature of the incident?

READER A: In some situations, with some individuals, I find it quite reasonable to blow my top--or at least let off a little steam.

READER G: But not with a woman. In that situation, if you are a man, it's usually wiser to under-react. Just grin and bear it. Or else leave the scene.

READER A: Or take a cold shower .

READER F: Once we assemble and arrange all this information about ourselves, how do we use it? What do we do next?

READER L: The next step would be to prioritize the items in Phase I. Place the things you are most interested in or concerned with at the top of the list and the others further down.

Then pick an item (not necessarily the first one on the list), examine it and think about how you are handling it at present. Assess what's good about it and what is not.

Determine how you would like it to be--in clear and specific terms. Then, if you think you might pursue this as a goal, list what you'll need in the way of money, muscle, skill, planning, decision making, moral courage, and so forth. Next, review what assets and qualities you have that will supply what is needed to reach your goal. Also, review your liabilities and weakness that might stand in your way.

Make a note of outside help that you might need. Then map out a plan and proceed with it.

READER D: What if you conclude that the goal you're seeking isn't worth the effort and commitment required to achieve it?

READER L: That's your decision. You can decide to proceed toward your goal or leave the matter as it is. Or you can try to eliminate it as an item of concern.

AUTHOR: Well stated, Reader L. And I think we can use your suggestions as the basis for the final phase of our project, with a little help from the Professor.

READER B: And here it is:

PHASE VI

HOW TO USE THIS REVIEW TO IMPROVE YOUR LIFE

Step 1. Arrange all items listed in Phase I in the order of their importance to you. In other words put the things you are most interested in or concerned with at the top of the list. And those you are less interested in or concerned with further down the list.

Step 2. Over a period of time, examine thoroughly each item listed. On a particular item, assess all the pluses and minuses relating to it. Assess the way you are presently handling it.

If you think you'd like to do better with it, assess what is needed in the way of money, planning, decision making, moral courage, emotional energy and so forth. Then review what assets and qualities you have that will supply what is needed.

Also, review the liabilities and weaknesses you have that you might have to overcome. Make a note of any outside help you might need. Then, map out a plan and proceed with it.

On some items you may find that what it takes in effort and commitment to solve a particular problem or achieve a particular goal is more than you are willing to expend. That is for you to decide.

Benefits to be gained from examining your life include: increased self-awareness and understanding; help in coping with problems; help in achieving goals; and a better perspective on how you fit into the scheme of things. The knowledge and understanding gained should help clear the mind and give you the feeling of having more control over your life.

Chapter 13

READER F (artist):   Hm-m.   I've just made a cursory examination of my life.   If ambition, planning, goal setting, and decision making are prerequisites for a successful and worthwhile life, then mine must be a disaster.

READER C (aerobics instructor): Is it a disaster?

READER F: Well, I've never given it much thought.   But what could be better than doing what you like to do and getting paid for it.   Once at an art festival I was sketching an attractive young woman and a bystander remarked, "That's a heck of a way for a grown man to make a living--sitting around all day drawing pretty women."

And the other day, a friend asked me how it felt to have paintings and drawings hanging up in various places.   I told him it felt pretty good.

READER C: And you say you never had the ambition to be an artist?

READER F: I've always had an impulse to draw and paint-- a desire to do art but not necessarily to be an artist.   As for decision making or goal setting, since I do mostly commissions, I don't have to worry about what to paint or draw.

READER C: How about the other areas of your life?   Your personal life?

READER F: Same thing.   I've always gone along with what my family, my teachers, and my friends expected of me.   I just go with the flow.

READER C: Doesn't that mean giving up control of your life to other people?

READER F: Not completely.   There's a lot of people that are pretty good at telling other people how they should run their lives.   In fact, just about every day there might be several people telling me what I ought to be doing.   That may be a good thing, however, since I'm not much of a self-starter.   And I can still have control of my life, sort of, by choosing which advice to follow, which offer to accept, or which proposition to go along with.

READER L (business man): In other words, you do art but you don't do management.

READER F: You can say that again. As I said, I'm not much of a self-starter. Even the prints I sell are from pictures I did for someone else, as commissions. Some artists are just the opposite. They only paint what they want to paint and don't do commissions.

READER B (professor): I think it was John Singer Sargent who defined a portrait as a painting or drawing of someone done from a distance of five to seven feet and paid for by the sitter, or by the sitter's parents or guardian--with something a little wrong around the mouth.

READER F: I'll go along with that. Under circumstances other than that it's called a study.

READER L: How did you become a working artist? Didn't you have to set a goal and take steps to achieve it?

READER F: Not exactly. I had the desire to do art. I was always drawing. In high school I was the best at drawing portraits. But I never made a commitment. I never said my goal in life is to become an artist. And I never speculated on how to go about starting a career as an artist.

READER L: Then how did it come about? Did you just drift into it?

AUTHOR: Sort of. Shortly after I graduated from high school, my uncle fell and broke his hip and wanted me to take his place as a hotel clerk until his injuries healed. I said okay.

While I was working at the hotel, a portrait artist from New York came to town for several weeks and was painting portraits at a local department store. He stayed at the hotel and we became friends.

I showed him some of my work and he encouraged me and gave me a lot of tips on lighting and on the different techniques of charcoal, pastel, and oil painting. He said something to the effect that if you set up your easel they will come. And once you start doing it for money, you'll get serious about it and do it much better.

He was right. The following spring, someone from the high school called me and said that they were planning to have a Paris

Sidewalk Cafe theme for the Senior Prom and they would like for me to come set up my easel, wear a beret, and sketch charcoal portraits. They said that I could charge the sitters.

It went well. I was still sketching when the band played *Home Sweet Home*. That led to commissions and invitations to sketch at arts and craft festivals and, eventually, to my own studio. I am essentially a portrait artist. I do portraits of people, portraits of their pets, their homes, their churches, and their favorite landmarks.

About the only thing I do for my own gratification are minimalist abstract paintings. I try to see how simple I can be and still come up with an interesting and satisfying painting.

READER B: I've heard some other type artists refer to portrait painters as prostitutes because they paint to please their customers instead of themselves.

READER F: An abstract expressionist once accused me of being that and a bystander asked him: If portrait painting is prostitution, what would you call abstract expressionism? Masturbation?

READER D: How would you characterize your minimalist paintings?

READER F: What I'm attempting to achieve is pure artistic perfection where configuration, color and the arrangement of dark and lights all work together to create a unique, artistic entity.

READER D: I see. You're trying to play God. God created such perfect things as roses, oak trees, blue birds, tigers, sunsets, and so forth. And you are trying to come up with something unique and equally perfect and beautiful. Right?

READER F: I started doing them just as an exercise in dividing space, in harmonizing colors, and in placement of forms in relation to the edges of the canvas and to imaginary center lines, and to imaginary diagonals running between opposite corners of the canvas.

READER D: You just lost me. Maybe you can explain what you just said. But, first, tell us: What is the most important thing in a painting or drawing or in any piece of two dimensional art? What are you most concerned with?

AUTHOR: Excuse me. Seems to me that Reader D is in search of a bit of primal knowledge. If so, let's begin the search in the usual way by naming all types of two-dimensional art.

READER F: Well, there's drawing, which is anything done in black and white or shades of gray, or with a single dark earth color such as umber or burnt sienna. Paintings usually have more than one color. A sketch is a quickly and loosely done drawing or painting.

READER B: Other types of two-dimensional art are mosaics and stained glass. Tapestry and weaving.

READER L: Do we include photographs?

READER F: Yes. Also, advertising layouts, posters, billboards, road signs. Anything two-dimensional, I would think.

AUTHOR: Okay. Now, let's start peeling away the embellishments and the non-essentials of two-dimensional art and see if we can determine what is basic and common in every kind of two-dimensional art.

READER C: We can start by eliminating objectivity. A painting or drawing does not have to have recognizable objects in it.

READER B: Right. And it isn't necessary to use pure spectrum colors. Most pictures are done in toned down colors or in black and white or shades of gray.

READER D: However, there are works of art where only pure primary or spectrum colors are used, with no black or white or shades of gray.

AUTHOR: The prime question, then, is: What does a black and white picture have in common with one done in shades of gray, or with one done in muted colors, or with one done in pure colors?

READER F: I know what it is. My art teachers taught me about it and about how important it is in composing a picture.

AUTHOR: Don't tell us. Let's see if we can figure it out ourselves. It probably has to do with the arrangement of the colors or forms on a two-dimensional surface.

READER F: You're getting warm.

READER C: In chapter three we found that writing is basically an arrangement of symbols representing accented and unaccented or loud and soft sounds. So maybe a picture is an arrangement of loud and muted colors.

READER F: Good thinking but no cigar. A picture can be composed of all bright colors or all muted colors.

I'll give you a hint. Let's say black is the darkest shade of gray and white is the lightest shade of gray. What is the difference between white and black?

READER B: Black absorbs all colors and white reflects all colors.

READER F: Yes, but what is the visual difference?

READER D: By George, I think I've got it! A light bulb just switched on above my head. Every picture is an arrangement of dark and light colors, whether it's done in pure colors right out of the tube, mixed colors, shades of gray, or pure black and white.

READER F: Bingo. It's called the value composition--the arrangement of darks and lights. And without a good value composition your picture may appear off balance, stiff, boring, or just plain blah.

AUTHOR: How can an average gallery goer, or an artist for that matter, tell whether or not a picture has a good value composition. And if a picture appears stiff, off balance, boring or blah, how do we determine what's wrong with it?

READER A: Yeah. Suppose I'm trying to impress my friends or a prospective customer with my knowledge of art. If we're looking at a picture and I remark that the value composition is bad, what do I say if they ask me to explain my criticism?

READER F: The most often made mistake in value composition is when all the colors are about the same value. This occurs more often in muted color work. I've seen some pictures so bad, in that respect, that when they're photographed in black and white all you see is a gray blur. If you back away from such a picture and look at it through squinted eyes you'll get the same blurred effect. There is no dynamics in a picture like that. It's very blah.

READER A: I think I understand that point. What else is there?

READER F: Well, if you really want to impress someone, even experts, you use the Reader F theory.

READER B: And what might that be?

READER F: It's something that came about when I started doing those minimalist paintings that I mentioned earlier. This theory might be the most significant idea in design to come down the pike since the golden section theory. Most of the good artists and designers seem to use it, perhaps instinctively, but I have never heard it articulated by anyone and I have never read anything relating to it.

READER B: Are you going to reveal this great theory to us?

READER F: Sure. The part of the theory that applies to value composition is this: The greater the difference in light value of one area of a design to another area, the more of one you need than the other.

For example, if you were designing a black and yellow plastic watering can, how much black would you use to go with the much lighter yellow?

READER C: I would use an inch or so of black around the bottom and perhaps make the sprinkler part black and all the rest yellow.

READER F: What if you were using light yellow and light green

READER C: In that case I might use more equal amounts of each maybe forty percent light green and sixty percent light yellow or vice versa.

READER A: If it's okay to use sixty/forty with the yellow and green, why wouldn't it be right to use the same proportion with yellow and black?

READER C: Because, to me, that would be an ugly combination.

READER F: It's okay to use equal amounts in small areas of a painting. But about the only time it's used broadly is in advertising, where the idea is to grab your attention, or in such things as the checkered flag at the race track where, again, the object is to grab your attention.

READER A: I once saw a painting hanging in a gallery that had only one solid color covering the whole canvas. Nothing else.

READER B: Was it interesting?

READER A: About as interesting as it would be for a musician to play one long continuous note on a horn and call it music.

READER C: Why would anyone waste time and materials on something like that?

READER A: Maybe he got a grant from the National Endowment for the Arts.

READER F: I've done pictures with just two colors or with two or more values of one color. But that is as minimal as I get.

READER B: I've seen drawings on white paper using only a few skimpy black lines--with far less than one percent black to white. Yet they seemed okay.

READER F: Yes. It doesn't matter how little an amount of one value you use in relation to another value.

READER B: Suppose I'm doing a painting using several different colors--let's say two dark colors, with one slightly darker than the other and a third color that is much lighter--how should I handle it?

READER F: In that case the two darker colors could occupy similar or dissimilar amounts of space in the picture. However, the much lighter color should occupy a lot less space than the other two combined or a lot more.

Let's say you're designing a man's tie--a striped tie. One way to go would be to have the dark color stripes be an inch or so wide and the light color just a narrow pinstripe between the other two.

Or, you could have the main color be the light color and use the dark colors as pinstripes or as small repeated designs.

For a free-form design you might use thirty percent of the light color, five percent of the darkest color and sixty-five percent of the other color.

AUTHOR: You implied earlier that your theory might apply to other elements of two-dimensional art.

READER F: Right. Although I'm still evaluating this, it might be that the greater the difference in the texture of two areas of a picture, the more you need of one than the other.

Or, the greater the difference in intensity of two colors, the more you need of one than the other.

Or, the greater the difference in configuration of two forms, the more you need of one than the other. For instance, in a landscape with a barn in it, the barn has a boxy configuration while the rest of the landscape has an organic and irregular configuration. If you want to feature the barn, have it take up most of the space. But if you want a general landscape, have the barn occupy just a small portion of the picture.

READER D: Very interesting. Earlier you said something about the placement of forms in relationship to center lines and diagonal lines running between opposite corners of the canvas.

READER F: Well, the object of a painting is to entertain us visually. In order to do that the eye of the viewer must be kept moving around the surface of the picture? One way to achieve this is through the use of asymmetry. Never center a form on a center line or on one of the diagonals. This tends to stop the movement of the eye and that area of the painting becomes a dead spot.

And do not have any lines in your picture running along a center line, either across or up and down, or along one of the diagonals. For instance, if you are painting a seascape, do not have the horizon running along the exact middle of your canvas. Place it above or below the center. Pretend that your canvas is a pool table and that if you run a line toward a corner pocket or a side pocket it will lead your eye right out of the picture. But at any other point your eye will rebound back into the picture.

Does that make any sense to you?

READER D: Very much so. With a few more pointers, I could include art reviewing in my prospective new career. What else in the way of inside stuff do I need to learn about?

READER F: Color. Color schemes and color harmony. There are two main categories of color harmony--analogous harmony and complementary harmony.

Analogous harmony is achieved by using colors that are side by side on the color wheel. For example, if you wanted the principle color to be yellow, colors analogous to yellow are orange and green. This makes for a pleasant, naturally harmonious, color scheme. It becomes more harmonious if you add a little yellow to the other two colors. And even more harmonious if you add a little dab of each color to each other color.

Complementary colors are colors that are opposite each other on the color wheel, such as yellow and violet, or red and green, or blue and orange. They are not naturally harmonious to each other. In fact, they are dissonant. To make them harmonious, or less dissonant, add some of each to the other or add black or white.

The three primary colors, red, yellow, and blue, are neither harmonious nor dissonant with each other. To make them harmonious, add some of each to each other or add black or white.

Pure, undiluted colors aren't used too often by artists except in advertising or for signs, logos, emblems, flags and so forth, where the object is to grab the viewer's attention and not necessarily to give the viewer a meaningful aesthetic experience.

Color has three qualities. The first is hue, such as red, yellow, blue, brown, avocado, azure, black, white, coral, gray, and so forth.

The second quality is its light or dark value. Yellow has a light value--purple has a dark value. You can change the value of any color by adding white to make it lighter or black to make it darker.

The third quality is intensity. Pure spectrum or rainbow colors--red, orange, yellow, green, blue and violet are the most intense. You can dull the intensity of a color by adding some of its opposite color, red to green, yellow to violet, blue to orange, or vice versa. You can also reduce the intensity of a color by adding white, black, or neutral gray.

READER D: A long time ago, someone told me that if you have a tube of pure blue, a tube of pure red, and a tube of pure yellow, along with black and white, that you can duplicate any color using just those basic colors. Is that true?

READER F: It's true, depending on the purity of your pigments and on how good you are at mixing them.

AUTHOR: That's remarkable. Can you tell us how you go about matching a color?

READER C: Down at the paint store they do it with a computerized machine.

READER F: Yes, but in quantities of a gallon or more.

READER D: Suppose I'm painting a still life that has a pair of my brown leather gloves in it. How would I mix that particular shade of brown from red, blue, and yellow colors and black and white?

READER F: First ask yourself which primary color is brown most like. Is it more like yellow? Is it more like red? Or is it more like blue?

READER D: I guess it would be closest to red.

READER F: Are your gloves a reddish brown or could the color have a little yellowish tint?

READER D: It appears to be reddish brown.

READER F: Okay. To make reddish brown you start with red and add some of its opposite color, which is green. You don't have any green, so you have to make some by mixing the two other primary colors, yellow and blue. Then you add the green, a small amount at a time, until you get reddish brown.

But you are not quite through. Next, you compare the color you have mixed with the color of your glove. Ask yourself--is the glove darker than the color you've mixed or is it lighter?

If the glove is darker, add a little black to your mixture. If the glove is lighter, add white.

Finally, you compare again for intensity. If your mixture is a bit too reddish, tone it down by adding a little more green. If it's too dull, compared with the glove, add a little more red.

READER C: What if the gloves were more of a yellowish brown?

READER F: In that case, you'd start with orange, a mixture of yellow and red. And you'd use the remaining color blue as your modifier.

READER C: This sounds fascinating. It's something I would like to learn and be able to teach to my kids.

READER F: You may still be able to buy basic watercolor sets that have only the three primary colors and black and white. I've taught my nieces and nephews how to make colors using that set. I had them snip patches of color from a magazine and try to duplicate the colors.

AUTHOR: Are there other facets of painting and drawing that Reader D might need to know about in order to become an art reviewer?

READER F: He could gain a lot by taking an art appreciation course at a nearby college and learning about the history of art and about the different movements and developments that have come about.

READER A: Question. What's the difference between traditional art and modern? Is it that traditional is realistic and modern art is abstract? If so, I'm confused, because some so-called modern art looks fairly realistic to me. Especially Cezanne's.

READER F: You might say that all art is abstract. If you are out painting a landscape, for instance, you're reducing a three-dimensional reality to a two-dimensional image. That's abstraction.

READER D: Ver-r-y interesting. So-called realistic art is produced by reducing objective reality to two-dimensional abstraction.

If that's the case, then true realistic art is when the artist converts non-objective images from his imagination into two-dimensional reality. Right?

READER F: You have a point.

READER B: Back to Reader A's question: What is the difference between traditional and modern art? If it's not realism versus abstraction, objectivity versus non-objectivity then what is it?

READER F: I think that traditional art has to do with the depiction of people, places, things, and events--actual or fictional--in a more or less natural and detailed manner, modified or enhanced by the aesthetic sensibilities of the artist and by his emotional involvement with the subject.

Modern artists may use people, places, and things as subjects but are less concerned with detailed objectivity and more concerned with creating poetic or dramatic arrangements of color and form and with expressing the feelings of the artist. Paul Cezanne has been called the father of modern art. Some of his pieces are virtual symphonies of color and form.

READER B: Cezanne was aware that his approach was different. He said of himself: "I am the primitive of a new art."

AUTHOR: If modern art is less objective, on the whole, than traditional, is it fair to say that traditional is less subjective than modern?

READER F: On balance, perhaps--However, between a Rembrandt painting and one by Cezanne, I couldn't say which is more subjective.

READER B: If you were to make such a judgement, it would be a subjective call. Right?

READER F: No doubt. The way I see it, you can measure objectivity in a painting by the square inch But subjectivity is measured by the depth of thinking, imagination, emotional involvement, and critical judgement that the artist brings to his work.

Chapter 14

READER L (business man): I was fascinated with the discussion, in the previous chapter, about color. Especially in regard to the pure spectrum colors that we see in a rainbow and about the infinite number of colors that can be made by mixing various combinations of the primary colors, red, blue, and yellow, along with black and white.

I've often heard that colors can affect our emotions and that prolonged dark cloudy weather or the short daylight hours of winter makes some people depressed. On the other hand sunshine and bright lights can cheer people up.

I'm curious. How much connection is there between color and the human spirit or human emotion? When God sends us a rainbow is he also sending us a message? A clue to our spiritual make-up? As in color, are there three primary emotions and three secondary emotions?

AUTHOR: You may be on to something. We often use color to describe our moods, with such terms as "feeling blue," or "tickled pink," or "green with envy," or "turning purple with rage."

READER F (artist): Before we get too far into this, we should realize that there is a difference in pigment colors, that artists use, and colored light, such as is used in television. In the latter, the primary colors are closer to orange, green, and violet and your secondary colors are yellow, blue, and red. For example, with light, to produce yellow you mix orange and green.

READER L: Good point. However, let's proceed with the use of red, blue, and yellow as the primaries. If need be, we can rectify the results later on.

READER F: Another thing to remember is, that with light, you get white by mixing all the spectrum colors together in the right proportion. But when you mix the same pigment colors together, you get something closer to black.

READER L: Why is that?

READER F: Well, when you see something painted red, for instance, what you see is red light reflected from pigment. The rest of the light falling on it is absorbed. Now, if you mix red with green, in the right proportion, the green pigment absorbs the red light and the red pigment absorbs the green light. And when all light is absorbed, a surface appears black. The same thing happens when you mix all the color pigments together.

READER L: I think there's a message somewhere in that phenomenon.

READER D: (couch potato): Okay, so when we look at an apple, we don't actually see the apple. What we see is light reflected from it. The source of that light is the sun, either directly or indirectly, the apple is of the earth but it is made visible by something from beyond the earth.

So, maybe the characteristics of a human soul can be determined by the kind of spiritual energy it reflects. The source of that energy is God, either directly or from the Godly spirit that is stored in his creations, in animals, plants, the ocean, the clouds, and in inspired works of human art, human action, and in the creeds and practices of religious institutions and other institutions.

If an object is black, it does not reflect light. It absorbs the light and turns it into heat. If enough heat builds up in an object it will melt down, evaporate, burst into flame, or explode. The energy becomes destructive of the object and of things nearby. But if a proper outlet can be devised for that energy the object will not be destroyed and the energy can be converted back to light, or to mechanical energy, or to usefully directed heat.

Similarly, If a human soul is dark, spiritual energy is not reflected, but is absorbed and turned into anxiety. If enough anxiety builds up in a human soul, it also becomes destructive of itself and of other souls unless this energy of anxiety can be channeled into good and useful activities.

AUTHOR: How does this spiritual energy come to us?

READER D: According to the New Agers it comes in the form of vibrations.   There are good vibrations and bad vibrations, they say. The way I would put it is that each thing in our environment and each activity that occurs has a certain spiritual quality emanating from it. We pick up on this through the senses of smell, sight, taste, hearing, and touch, and maybe another sense or two that we are not conscious of. If we give our attention to something beautiful, a vase of fresh cut gladioli for example, the spirit of gladiolus is picked up by our eyes and if we are mentally healthy that spirit will be directed to a pleasure center of the brain and cause joy molecules to be released, which speed to receptors in the cells of the body and makes us feel good all over.

A kind word from someone or an appropriate pat on the back can have a similar effect. So can a particular piece of music, or the taste of a favorite food, or the laughter of children, or petting a puppy.

On the other hand, if we give our attention to something mean, odious, undesirable, ugly or unkind, the bad spirit from it will be directed to a center of the brain that will cause us to feel anger, sorrow, hate, emotional pain or anxiety. We can alleviate these unpleasant feelings by dealing in a positive, constructive way with whatever is causing the anger, the pain, or the anxiety.

AUTHOR: Generally speaking, anxiety and other unpleasant emotions come from having to face life. When some problem comes up that we have to deal with, or when something in our life is not the way we'd like it to be, or when we are threatened by something, or when we desire something that is not forthcoming, anxiety builds up and our mood darkens. If we can come up with a way to resolve the source of the anxiety, in a successful and socially acceptable way, then our mood becomes lighter and the anxiety goes away.

READER B {professor}: I agree. For example, when we are threatened by something, a mugger let's say, the anxiety we feel is called fear. Fear gets the adrenaline flowing and prepares us for flight or fight. Sometimes flight may be the most satisfactory way to resolve the situation. Other situations require that we stand and fight or pursue and attack. When we do this, fear is converted to courage and if we are successful in dealing with a dangerous threat, it can lighten the spirit considerably, sometimes to the point of exhilaration.

On the other hand, if we become immobilized or frozen with fear and unable to run or fight, things can look very dark.

READER D: When the prudent thing to do is run, fear is changed to discretion.

READER A (insurance man): I think most people would agree that fear is one of the basic emotions. Let's say it's one of the three primary emotions. If so, which primary color would you assign to it?

READER C (aerobics instructor): How about yellow? When someone acts cowardly, we say he's yellow or that he has a yellow streak down his back.

READER B: Not necessarily. A person we refer to as yellow might be someone with an adrenaline deficiency, who can't generate enough courage to fight. He's a lightweight in that area but may be very good at avoiding danger or confrontation.

I think red would be a more suitable color. Red flags and red traffic lights are designed to scare us into stopping. And when a temperature gauge or a battery gauge swings over into the red zone, or when a red warning light comes on, it is to scare us into doing whatever needs to be done.

On the courage side, we say that a courageous person is red-blooded or that he wears the red badge of courage.

READER A: Yellow is one of the primary colors, so if it doesn't represent fear-slash-courage, what emotion does if represent?

READER D: The yellow traffic light tells us to be cautious, to look around and assess the situation and determine whether we should stop, proceed with caution, or hurry across the intersection before the light changes to red.

AUTHOR: Wouldn't that have more to do with intelligence than with emotion?

READER D: Well, if it takes fear to make us run or fight, then there should be an emotion that urges us to look, listen, taste, smell, or feel and to shed light on a situation.

READER B: I think the emotion we're looking for is curiosity or wonder. Curiosity is the driving force that causes us to assess a situation, or to look for information, or to seek enlightenment. Wonder is expressed passively by giving our attention to what is before us.

AUTHOR: If curiosity makes us want to shed light on things, then it should be represented by yellow, the lightest primary color.

READER M (philosophy teacher): You people are amazing. I don't know how much validity there is in what you've come up with, but you make it sound quite plausible. The same thing, I suppose, could be said about Plato's writings. What he had to say may not have been absolute truth, but the way he said it was so convincing and effective that he's been called the inventor of western civilization.

Now, I'm anxious to learn about the third primary emotion, to be represented by blue, the remaining primary color.

READER D: It has got to be DESIRE. Curiosity causes us to look around. When we do so, we might see something that threatens us and arouses fear in us. On the other hand, we might see something attractive that arouses a feeling of desire. Desire is expressed by reaching out, in one way or another, for the object of our desire. I think it is a primary emotion because it is necessary for survival.

READER A (insurance man): What if you reach out for something you desire and someone stops you or tries to make things difficult for you?

READER D: That's when you need courage. Desire will inspire you to reach for something, but it requires courage to follow through and take or win the object of your desire, in the face of opposition.

READER M: Again, I find it hard to disagree. Let's see, we have our three primary selections. Now, we need three more emotions to complete our spiritual rainbow. They will be represented by the three secondary colors, orange, green and violet. Any suggestions?

READER D: Perhaps we can get an idea from opposites on the color wheel. Let's see. The opposite or complementary of blue is orange. Blue is desire, which has to do with wanting things we don't have or wanting to do things that we are not doing. Maybe the emotion we are looking for in the orange slot, has to do with how we feel about the things that we have, or the things we are doing, or with what's happening. Would that be pleasure or pain, joy or sorrow, euphoria or despair?

READER A: Sounds right to me. Joy is expressed by smiling, laughing and so forth. Sorrow and displeasure are expressed by, crying, moaning, groaning, or griping.

READER M: I'm sure there are some who would question your logic in all this, but you make it seem apt and believable.

READER B: Perhaps logic doesn't have anything to do with it. Maybe it has to do with art. Could it be that the stuff we've come up with is the result of collective creativity on our part?

READER M: Your observation sounds logical to me. Now let's have a little creative thinking about green or violet. What emotion does either of these represent on our spiritual rainbow?

READER E (young religious woman): Using Reader D's method, maybe we can determine the emotion for the violet slot by studying its opposite on the color wheel. The opposite of violet is yellow, which represents curiosity and wonder. Curiosity and wonder are expressed by seeking to know or experience new things through the five senses.

Faith has to do, somewhat, with clear thinking about our experiences and about our knowledge of things--knowledge already gained through the senses.

It also has to do with things not seen, with a kind of knowledge or vision that does not come from direct experience.

Example. When you flick a light switch to the on position you have faith that your light will come on because it has done so thousands of times before. That is clear constructive thinking based on experience.

Example two. If you are a devout Christian, you believe that by asking God to forgive your sins and by accepting Jesus Christ as your Savior, that you will go to heaven, although you have no proof that this will happen. But through faith you hold a clear thought that it will happen.

READER M: To reiterate, faith is expressed through clear thinking or by holding on to a clear thought, idea, or vision. What is the purpose of faith? How is it used?

READER E: In Matthew 17:20, Jesus said to his disciples, "If ye have faith as a grain of mustard seed, ye shall say to yonder mountain; remove hence to yonder place; and it shall remove; and nothing shall be impossible to you."

READER L (business man): I agree that faith is characterized by clear thinking and vision. But to get results you have to add work. If you don't bestir yourself to flip on the switch, that light won't come on. And if you don't get busy with a pick and shovel or with bulldozers and earth movers, you're not going to move that mountain.

READER E: James 2:26, "For as the body without the spirit is dead, so faith without works is dead also."

READER M: Okay. Faith is expressed through vision and by clear, constructive thinking, and by supporting, promoting, and working for the object of your faith. What happens if faith is lost, broken, or suppressed?

READER C: When faith is broken or suppressed it changes to doubt, which is expressed by worrying and by unconstructive thinking, murky vision, and by a reduced ability to function effectively or to cope with the object of your worry.

READER A: The big question is how do you change doubters into believers? How do you make a worrier stop staring at the ceiling or running around in circles and get him or her to focus on the problem, examine the situation, and start thinking constructively?

READER D: If someone is hysterical you give 'em a sharp slap on the side of the face. For something less than hysteria you give a psychological equivalent of a slap in the face, the purpose of which is to stop the person from mentally running around in circles and to get him back on track.

READER C: Prevention, of course, is the best cure. To prevent a person from becoming a worrier requires inoculation at a very early age, preferably by examples of how parents and other family members successfully deal with every day problems that arise or with crises and disappointments that come along.

READER E: One of the best ways to turn off the worry machine is by the use of prayer. When we ask God for guidance to lead us out of darkness and into the light, or when we pray for

135

forgiveness of our sins, or when we pray for strength to bear our burdens. He usually comes through, sometimes in a miraculous way.

AUTHOR: A person who prays and worships God is referred to as a believer. Should we then refer to an atheist as a doubter?

READER E: That might be appropriate or you could call him a non-believer, or one who believes there is no God. But it doesn't matter what you call him, he's still negative to the idea that there is a supreme being with a higher intelligence than ours.

AUTHOR: Which do you think would be easier to convert to a believer an atheist or an agnostic?

READER E: Well, if, as mentioned earlier, doubt is suppressed faith, then it would seem to me that the atheist has the best potential for becoming a believer. His denial of the existence of God indicates to me that he's at least thinking about it.

As for the agnostic, he might not think much about it one way or the other--or care.

READER A: I wonder how much difference there is in the way agnostics, atheists, and believers conduct their lives. Is one group more moral than the others? More charitable? More intelligent? More successful?

READER M: That would make an interesting subject for a survey, no doubt. Meanwhile, back to our rainbow of emotions. We still have the green slot left.

READER A: I've read or heard many times that anger is a basic emotion. Rage is an extreme form of anger. Envy, jealousy, and hate are related to anger and rage, in that they all are destructive in one way or another.

READER C: It seems to me that we haven't mentioned the most important emotion of all. It is one that definitely belongs in that rainbow.

READER D: Let me guess. Ah yes, I think I've got it. It's "what the world needs now." It is "a many splendored thing." It's a "warm puppy." It's the opposite of hate. If I were playing Jeopardy, my answer would be, "What is this thing called love?"

Everybody talks about loving this or that or about doing one thing or another for love, or that love is the answer for whatever is wrong in our lives or in the world. But what is it exactly? What are its characteristics? How does it work? Why is it so difficult to get it right?

READER M: The last serious discussion on the subject took place over two thousand years ago. According to Plato, a bunch of friends got together one night in Athens for an evening of drinking, eating, and conversation that resolved into a symposium on love.

As usual, Plato has Socrates dominating the dialogue. Socrates begins by saying that he learned about love from a woman named Diotima, who was from a place called Mantinea.

Her first point was that love is the intermediary between God and mortals. Between Heaven and Earth. It is a mean between our earthly appetites and activities on the one hand and true pure love, along with the absolutes of beauty, truth, and goodness, on the other hand.

She defined human love as the desire for everlasting possession of the beautiful, the good and the true.

READER A: Love is a desire? I thought love and desire were two different emotions.

READER M: You have a point. And unless we clear up the matter it could muddy the colors in our rainbow. We can desire to feel the emotion of love just as we can desire to eat strawberries. But desiring strawberries and enjoying the eating of them isn't the same thing.

READER A: So how do we experience this thing called love?

READER M: Well, as Plato said, it has to do with the beautiful, the good, and the true. So maybe we can take off from there and update and elaborate on his ideas.

READER K (retired farmer): Speaking of strawberries, if I say I love wild strawberries, can that be a valid statement? Should I say instead that I enjoy wild strawberries?

READER M: Let me ask this. Do you also love bananas?

READER K: I like them, but I wouldn't say I love them.

READER A: So how did this love affair between you and strawberries come about?

READER K: Well, the first time I remember eating them was after we moved out to that farm when I was seven years old. One spring day, my father was plowing a piece of land in preparation for planting corn. I was over on the edge of the field, looking around and enjoying the sunshine and the birds singing when I discovered these bright red berries. I asked my dad about them and he told me what they were and that they were good to eat. I tasted them and I thought they were the best tasting thing I'd ever eaten. And they were just growing there. You didn't have to go to the store to get them. I'll never forget that day as long as I live. Every time I eat strawberries, even those I buy at the stores, I'm reminded of it.

READER M: Do you remember the first time you ate bananas?

READER K: I can't say that I do.

READER E: Perhaps on some level he realized that strawberries are a beautiful gift created and given to us by a higher power.

READER M: Evidently the strawberries, along with the singing of the birds and the beauty of a spring day caused him to feel the emotion of love.

So let's update Plato's definition by saying, that in one sense, love is the emotion we can feel when we witness, or when we are the recipient of , the beautiful, the good, and the true.

READER A: What if he had eaten too many of the strawberries and had become sick?

READER M: Eating too many of the berries would have been out of harmony or out of order with the spirit of love.

READER B: Let me rephrase and add to our definition. Love is the emotion we can feel when we witness, experience, or receive something having the qualities of beauty, order, harmony, wellness, truth, and goodness, as long as there is no conflict with the established beauty, order, harmony, wellness, truth and goodness.

READER C: I don't think that covers it completely. It's too passive. Isn't there an active side to love, on our part, where we actively create, promote, or express beauty, order, harmony, wellness, truth, and goodness?

READER M: How right you are.

READER B: Okay, how's this? Love is the emotion that we can feel and express by creating, promoting, giving, receiving, or experiencing, beauty, order, harmony, wellness, truth, and goodness, in a way that does not conflict too much with the established beauty, order, harmony, wellness, truth, and goodness.

READER A: Could you elaborate on the part about not conflicting with the established beauty, order, and so forth?

READER B: Okay. For example, if I kiss my wife and we both enjoy it and find it meaningful, that's love. We should sip it up like wine. However, if I kiss somebody else's wife, even though there might be some momentary pleasure, eventually, it might cause the whole barrel of wine to turn to vinegar.

AUTHOR: Another example, if, after a busy day, I go out in the backyard, and enjoy smoking my pipe, while watching a beautiful sunset, that might be an act of love.

But if I were to go inside and smoke one pipeful of tobacco after another, around other people, that would not likely qualify as love.

READER C: That would be asphyxiation.

READER D: I think we get the picture. As we learned from the movie, Love Story, "Love is never having to say you're sorry." Everything we do has an everlasting effect. When we do something in the spirit of love the effect is one of everlasting good, and we'll never have to apologize for it.

The feeling that accompanies acts of love, whether we're on the receiving side or the giving side, is one of pleasure and meaning, with no unpleasant aftertaste.

READER L: Speaking of giving and receiving, some people are referred to as givers. They appear to give more than they receive. Mother Teresa, for example. Others are called takers because they seemingly take more than they give.

Question: Is giving always good and taking not so good?

READER C: Giving in the spirit of love is usually good, especially if the gift is thoughtful and is meaningful to the

139

recipient. However, ignoring the possible long-term effect of giving in a particular situation, is not in the spirit of love. Neither is giving something bad, or giving too much of a good thing.

As for taking, generally speaking, you should take only what is offered to you or what you've earned or paid for. If something is offered to you in the spirit of love and if you can see no long term bad consequences, then taking it is probably a good thing. But taking something that belongs to someone else and is not freely offered or taking something unearned or unpaid for is likely to be bad and not in the spirit of love.

AUTHOR: In other words, giving and taking is good when it fosters long-term beauty, order, harmony, wellness, truth, and goodness. And bad when it fosters the opposite. As Reader D said, the feeling that accompanies love is one of pleasure and meaning, with no bad aftertaste. What is the nature of that good? Is there a specific area of the brain where the feeling originates or a specific molecule produced by the brain that carries this feeling to the cells of the body? Or does it come directly from God in an immaterial form?

READER A: It probably has something to do with the area of the brain that was discussed in chapter two, concerning the experiment with the mouse and concerning reader F's euphoric experience. The molecules that convey the feeling to the body cells are probably the endorphins we talked about in chapter one.

READER R: I've just re-read an article on endorphins, authored by Stephen S. Hall, that was printed in the June, 1989 Smithsonian Magazine. There's seven or more of these substances, believed to be produced by the brain. The effect they have on the body is that they reduce pain and induce a feeling of well being. The effect is similar to that produced by opium based drugs such as heroin and morphine.

One of the endorphins, called dynorphin, is two hundred times more powerful than commercial grade morphine and there are no bad side effects. It produces a natural high. I asked my druggist if morphine is chemically similar to dynorphin or does it just stimulate the body's production of endorphins. He said that the molecules are similar and work the some way. He also said that when you take opium based drugs your body stops producing the corresponding endorphin. If that happens and you lose access to the opium based drug, your high becomes the lowest of lows. You go from feeling heavenly to feeling like hell.

The natural high that comes from loving and being loved may not be as intense as a large shot of heroin, but it is more meaningful. And if the everyday give and take of life is conducted in the spirit of love, that high, I believe, can be maintained more or less constantly.

AUTHOR: Could you elaborate on the every day give and take thing?

READER B: Well, for me, that would mean getting up in the morning in time to have breakfast with my family, then hug and kiss them goodbye. Then drive safely and courteously to work. As a teacher, if I love my students, I will do my best to motivate them to learn and to think. I will not hug or kiss my students. And I'll grade them strictly on merit.

In another publication, I read that little things, such things as kind words, compliments, a pat on the back, a smile, or such things as petting your dog or cat, can release endorphins.

AUTHOR: Let's get this clear. Are you saying that if someone conducts his life in the spirit of love, on a regular basis, then he'll be supplied regularly with enough endorphins to maintain a more or less constant feeling of well being?

READER B: Something like that. Of course, at times, unpleasant situations will arise that can slow down the flow of endorphins, but if you are the lover type, you'll bounce back with far less difficulty.

On the other hand, if you are an ill-tempered, inconsiderate, self-centered, unloving person, interested only in instant gratification, you might feel a temporary high when satisfying some particular appetite, but it soon fades. Eventually, you'll wind up in a spiritual snake pit, feeling hate instead of love, revulsion instead of desire, doubt instead of faith, fear instead of courage, pain and sorrow instead of joy, and boredom instead of wonder.

READER D: From what you've said, I think we can put together a scientific definition of love.

READER B: A scientific definition?

READER D: Yes.   Love is anything that makes the endorphins flow and doesn't produce any bad side effects.

READER B: Not bad, but how do you determine, scientifically, what is a bad side-effect and what is not? It seems to me that deciding that involves subjective judgement, not scientific certainty.

READER D: You are correct, of course. I guess you can't define it scientifically. But that's probably a good thing. Taking the mystery and tentativeness out of the phenomenon of love might destroy it.

READER C: I remember reading that the release of endorphins is facilitated by another body chemical called serotonin and that some people do not produce a sufficient amount of serotonin, with the result that such people feel pain more sharply and are more easily depressed. Is the shortage due to their genetic makeup or is it the result of behavioral or environmental factors?

READER B: Good question. But it's one I can't answer.

READER D: I heard a caller on a radio talk show say that the reason he uses illegal drugs is because his body doesn't produce enough serotonin, making him more susceptible to depression.

READER C: Depression is now considered a biological illness and is treated as such by doctors with a number of drugs. It seems to me that prescription drugs, given under the care of a physician, would be cheaper and safer than illegal street drugs.

READER A: If love involves the distribution of endorphins to body cells and if serotonin is necessary in that process, then it seems to me that a person's capacity for love depends on how much serotonin he has. Ain't science wonderful! Now, when you sign up for a dating service, you can include your serotonin level along with the list of your hobbies, likes and dislikes, and other personal information.

Another thing. Most states require a blood test, before issuing a marriage license, to prevent the spread of disease. Next thing you know they'll start requiring serotonin tests to help reduce the divorce rate.

AUTHOR: One thing modern science is reducing, if not destroying altogether, is romance. For example, since we landed men on the moon, when have you heard the moon mentioned in a song or story, in a romantic way?

READER D: Not in a blue moon, I'd say.

READER L: I don't know how scientists or wise men rate on the love scale, but it's been said that "only fools fall in love." If that is true, thank God we still have plenty of them around.

AUTHOR: Question. Does anyone have anything to say about whether or not green is the appropriate color to represent love in our spiritual rainbow?

READER C: In nature the green in leaves is very much involved in creating all kinds of lovely things--flowers, trees, fruit, nuts, and thousands of other good things.

READER A: Green is the color of money, which can be traded for love.

READER D: On the negative side, when love is suppressed it turns into the dark dirty green of envy, jealousy and hate.

AUTHOR: Can't argue with any of that. Now that we've got our emotional rainbow completed, let's discuss the emotional or spiritual significance of black and white and shades of gray.

READER B: Before we proceed, there are a couple of things we need to consider. According to many psychologists, all emotional responses, except for the startle response, are learned and are not very consistent, and may be different in different cultures. For example, we in the western world usually associate death with the color black.   But many orientals associate it with white.

The reason we associate black with something bad is probably because more bad people do more bad things at night, under the cover of darkness. And dark stormy skies threaten us with thunder, and lightning, and floods, and leaky roofs.

On the other hand, we associate the whiteness of gently falling snowflakes or the beauty and stillness of a snow covered landscape with the highest and purist of spiritual feelings.

READER H (musician):   The dark emotions are not necessarily bad. They are probably the root source of the higher emotions. Like a bass note in music, that can energize a number

143

of higher harmonic overtones in the source instrument and resonate in other instruments as well.

The way I see it, there are three main categories or levels of emotion. First there is the carnal level that goes along with carnal appetites and drives. Some people, it seems, never get above this level. They are like alligators, only interested in eating, copulating, and destroying any other creature that enters their territory.

The second level is the sensual level where we develop appetites for sensual pleasures and activities beyond the carnal, such as for music, dancing, art, fancy foods, travel, nature, literature.

The third is the celestial level, representing the highest and purist level of the human spirit.

There are graduated levels in between these. Some music, such as heavy metal rock, gangsta rap, and gut bucket blues, might lean toward carnality. Big band music, musical comedy, and opera would reflect sensuality. And church hymns, Handel's Messiah, and Beethoven's ninth symphony evoke the higher spiritual emotions.

There are higher and lower levels in each category. For instance, sexual intercourse is a carnal activity. The lowest level of it is rape. Other levels are prostitution, and out of wedlock sex. The highest form is that between a happily married husband and wife, where it can run the gamut from carnal, through the sensual, and into the realm of high spirituality.

READER B: Interesting concept. Another example: The lowest form of ballroom dancing might be the lambada which dips well into the carnal. On the high side, the waltz has very little carnality and may lean a bit toward the spiritual. Although, when it first came upon the scene, it was considered vulgar.

READER A: In sports, boxing and football are in the blood and guts category and golf is up among the sublime.

READER M: I agree with Reader B that the concept is interesting. And it appears to be quite valid and applicable in a broad spectrum of human activity, even though the determinations are arrived at subjectively.

In the way of emotional responses, according to studies made by psychologist Eugen and others, there are three ways that emotional responses can be judged quite reliably and objectively. The response most easily judged is that of pleasantness or unpleasantness. Does a particular thing make the corners of your mouth turn up or turn down?

The second is attention or rejection. Does a thing hold your attention or do you turn away from it?

The third response is tension or sleep. Does something excite you or does if put you to sleep?

AUTHOR: Let's hope that our dialogue holds the attention of great numbers of readers and that they are pleased and excited by what we say.

We've discussed the emotions represented by our rainbow of colors and by black and white. But we haven't said much if anything about emotions represented by shades of gray or by colors modified by their opposites on the color wheel.

READER F: Medium gray is a neutral blend of all the spectrum colors with a balanced amount of black and white. Some people seem to have gray type personalities. Their emotional range is in shades of grey--the dark tones representing tenseness or anxiety and lighter tones release from tension and anxiety.

As for emotions represented by mixtures of opposites, that could get complicated. If we modify love, which is represented by green, by adding a bit of fear, represented by dark red, what do we come up with?

READER D: Weaker love, represented by a duller green.

READER F: Perhaps. However, I've heard that love has the power to change fear to courage. If that's true, you could call the result fortified love, represented by terre verte, a beautiful earth-green pigment.

For example, suppose you see a mugger attacking a sweet old lady, on your street. In the spirit of love, you would like to go to the aid of the woman, but the prospect of confronting the mugger stirs up fear in you. But if the spirit of love in you is strong enough, it might convert your fear to courage. And strengthened by this combination of love and courage, and perhaps a baseball bat, you subdue the mugger and turn him over to the police. That would be an act of fortified love on your part.

READER D: If I ever do such a good deed, I'll smile while I'm doing it so that the mugger will know that I'm hitting him in the spirit of love and not out of hate.

READER F: As I said, it does get complicated. However, modified emotions, like modified colors, are probably more interesting than the pure thing. Most artists blend their colors and try to create new combinations, new harmonic subtleties, and new dynamic arrangements of lights and dark, to more fully express their ideas and feelings.

Similarly, writers often create characters motivated by mixed or conflicting emotions because readers identify with them and find them more interesting than stereotypical or one-dimensional characters.

READER D: There are thousands upon thousands of blended colors in nature and in art. Colors such as coral, sepia, plum, fuchsia, peach, turquoise, all with their equivalent emotions. I wonder what emotion goes with robin's egg blue?

READER A: Deep down, it represents the desire to fly or sing like a bird.

AUTHOR: Earlier, the professor said that except for the startle response all emotional responses are learned. I suppose most of them are learned early in life. If a child grows up in an emotionally healthy environment he will learn to respond positively and constructively to life's situations. But if he grows up in a dysfunctional, emotionally sick environment, he will likely learn negative, unsatisfactory, and anti-social responses.

The big question is this. Can negative responses be unlearned? Can people of any age, no matter what their childhood environment was, acquire the ability to change the negative energy of anxiety into positive spiritual energy?

READER A: I don't see why not. If we can strengthen our muscles by pumping iron and improve our cardio-vascular system and general body health with proper exercise and diet, we should be able to become emotionally and spiritually healthy through appropriate exercises.

READER C: I agree. If a person can learn to paint pictures, or learn how to tap dance, or play a video game, he or she should be able to learn ways of using emotional energy positively and constructively.

AUTHOR: We've already discussed in a general way how to do that with the six basic emotions that make up our spiritual rainbow. Let's review them, now, and come up with specific ways to express and exercise them.

READER C: I'll go first, with the most important emotion. We said that LOVE is expressed by creating, promoting, or witnessing beauty, order, harmony, wellness, truth, and goodness. There are a million ways to do that. Be generous with smiles and compliments. Grow things. Bake a cake. Mow the lawn. Pick up trash. Make music. Send a check to the Salvation Army. Support your local symphony.

Talk to your children, to your spouse, to people in a check out line. And listen to them. Let them know that you think they are worthwhile members of the human race. When you do such things, you not only express love, you also feel it and cause others to feel it. It is a good feeling.

The reverse of love is envy, jealousy, and hate which is expressed by destroying good things and causing bad feelings.

READER D: DESIRE is expressed and can be aroused by reaching out. Reaching out with the hands is one way, either in a catching mode, a grasping mode, or in a palms up begging mode. Other ways of reaching out are with the eyes and ears, the telephone, or by letter writing. When it comes to arousing desire in people, advertising is probably the most successful way to do it.

The reverse of desire is revulsion, expressed by pushing away, holding your nose, closing or covering your eyes, stopping up your ears, or by saying no.

Excessive desire, especially for sex or power, is called lust. It is expressed by groping or grabbing.

The highest form of desire is a desire for spiritual oneness with God, with the universe, or with the Great Spirit, or the desire for nirvana. It is expressed through prayer, transcendental

147

mediation, smoking the peace pipe, taking holy communion and so forth.

READER M: I'll take wonder. WONDER or curiosity is expressed by giving our attention to whatever is before us or to whatever is going on around us. Also by seeking information and judgement, by assessing, ciphering, by seeking solutions to problems, and by sampling new things and new ideas.

The highest expression of curiosity occurs in the search for justice and for absolute truth and goodness.

Curiosity is expressed carnally by looking at pornography, gawking at automobile wrecks, watching a fight, or reading a murder story, or by watching certain segments of the evening news and other television programs.

The reverse of wonder is apathy or boredom which is expressed by inattention, yawning, or sleeping.

READER A: COURAGE, as we defined it, is expressed physically by standing and fighting when attacked or by pursing and subduing an attacker. And the highest expression of courage is in risking one's own life to protect someone else. On the same high plane is the courage to stand up for virtue, justice, and morality in the face of opposite popular opinion or peer pressure, or in the face of temptation to do otherwise.

The reverse of courage is fear, expressed by running away or by failing to move forward in the face of opposition. The noblest form of fear is expressed by running away from the temptation to do something bad.

READER E: FAITH is expressed by clear thinking and by commitment to and working for the object of your faith. The highest form of faith is expressed by long term commitment to and by working for that which is Holy--to God, truth justice, and goodness.

The lowest form of faith is commitment to the devil and in believing that a good life comes from selfishness and from instant gratification of carnal or sensual desires.

The reverse of faith is doubt, which is expressed by unproductive thinking, worry, and mentally going around in circles, or making mountains out of molehills, and by useless repetitive actions.

READER F: The remaining emotion, JOY, is expressed by smiling, laughing, and sometimes by sighing or by shedding tears. Joy is the feeling and reward that comes when we express positively the other emotions--love, faith, courage, desire, and wonder or when they are expressed to us, in positive ways, by others and by God and nature. This kind of joy is meaningful and long lasting.

The meaningless pleasure that comes from self-centered indulgence, instant gratification of carnal appetites, or from using drugs, soon fades, leaving feelings of emptiness and misery.

READER M: Studies show that different emotions and different appetites originate in different parts of the brain, rage in one place, hunger in another, sexual arousal in another, and euphoria in yet another. As mentioned earlier, except for the startle factor, most of our emotional responses and the accompanying behavior patterns are learned. However, many medical doctors now say that severe emotional problems, such as depression, or frequent outbursts of rage, or short attention span, irrational fears, and so forth, are caused by chemical imbalances and in many cases are being successfully treated with drug therapy. Some imbalances stem from physical trauma. But isn't it possible that in other cases, learned thought patterns could initiate the chemical imbalance, and that if these undesirable patterns could be put on hold and attention given to acquiring more desirable ones, that the imbalance could be rectified without drugs? If people can use will power to stop smoking or stop drinking alcohol, why can't they use it to regulate emotional responses and destructive behavior by learning new thought patterns?

READER D: As the old saying goes--where there's a will there's a way. For anyone wanting to orchestrate a more positive emotional life for themselves, perhaps our discussions here on the spiritual rainbow can help steer the way.

You say you'd like to stop plodding along in the murky shadows and start walking on the sunny side of the street? Check out of Heartbreak Hotel and move to Sunnybrook Farm?

Climb out of the snake pit and go frolic in strawberry fields? Leave Sin City and cross over the bridge to Virtue Village?

Well, we have come up with some pretty good ideas on how to go about it. So if you can muster up the determination to change spiritually from the negative to the positive, our discussions can show you how to do it.

In other words, if you've got the will, we've got the way.

AUTHOR: Well, I don't think we should claim, absolutely, that we've discovered the way to emotional or spiritual well being. Each individual must search out his own unique pathway, taking into consideration his background and his present emotional or spiritual situation.

One individual might need only to veer a little to the right or left to be headed in the right direction. Another might need to hack his way through an emotional jungle or navigate across the shifting sands of a spiritual desert. What we've come up with, I think, are new ideas that anyone seeking to improve his spiritual well-being can use as tools or equipment to build that pathway to happiness.

READER F: Question: Is will an emotion? If so, what is its composition? From which of our six basic emotions is it composed? What color is it?

READER A: It's purple.

READER D: And why do you believe it to be purple?

READER A: Because will is a combination of desire, faith, and courage. We said that desire is blue, faith is violet, and courage is red. So if you mix those colors together, with a little extra of red, you'll get purple.

AUTHOR: If the will has to do with desire, faith, and courage, perhaps the way has something to do with the other three basic emotions, wonder, joy, and love.

READER D: That seems logical. What would you call a mixture of those three emotions?

READER M: May I suggest enthusiasm? Nowadays, it usually means keen, positive interest. Originally, it meant divine inspiration.

READER A: That's it--enthusiasm. Now, what color would it be?

READER F: When you mix orange, yellow, and green, you get gold.

AUTHOR: To sum it up, if one can summon up the will to curb his negative impulses and his bad behavior, there's a way-- you might say a golden way--to achieve spiritual well-being. It is by seeking divine inspiration and acting on it positively and with intense interest.

READER K: I wonder if that's how the Samoans do it. It would be interesting to compare these ideas of ours with the reality of the Samoan way of life as it was when I was there fifty years ago. A way of life that was virtually free of mental or spiritual illness and of moral depravity.

AUTHOR: From what you told us about the Samoans, back in chapter seven, I think our ideas would overlay pretty well with the elements of their way of life and with their spiritual make up.

READER K: Incidentally, the name of their country is formed from two words, Sa, meaning sacred and moa, meaning core or center. They believe that Samoa is the spiritual center of the world. Up until the time the British took control of the islands away from Germany by force in 1914 (an action welcomed by the Samoans), the Samoan spirit manifested itself chiefly in, inter-island warfare, sometimes cousin against cousin. But, since then, they've directed that spiritual energy into peaceful, worthwhile pursuits and into spirited siva dancing and singing. If a whole society can change its nature from one that is prone to violence to one that is happy, peaceful and gentle, it seems to me an individual could do as much.

AUTHOR: Let's hope that our search here for primal knowledge and the points discussed in our dialogue will motivate some of our readers to do just that.

About the Author

Robert Rakestraw grew up on a farm. He is a U.S. Marine Corps veteran from World War II. He operated a dance school with his wife from 1946-1966, then worked as a music teacher from 1966-1972. He was a member of the Rome Symphony Orchestra from 1961 - 1995, playing the contrabass. He is also an inventor with 2 U.S. patents and has been a working artist (drawing and painting) since 1971.

www.ingramcontent.com/pod-product-compliance
Lightning Source LLC
Chambersburg PA
CBHW020515290526
45786CB00002B/605